harvest
vegetarian

harvest vegetarian

Includes Vegan and Gluten-Free Recipes

Adam de Ath

NEW
HOLLAND

Contents

Dreamy Desserts
& Tempting Treats   *119*

V = vegan or vegan option

G = suitable for gluten-free diets

Acknowledgements

Along the way I've been supported and encouraged by great friends and family, and in particular I would like to thank:

Barbara McIntyre, a mentor, long-time friend and qualified chef and TAFE teacher, Barbara has been an inspiring influence in the development and improvements of my cooking skills and played a crucial role in establishing Harvest Vegetarian Restaurant. I have the highest respect for Barbara and her wealth of knowledge and expertise—thank you my distant friend, you are always in my thoughts and a driving force on which to be modelled.

Michael Cokkaris—Management & Accounting—the best partner in life and business that I could ever ask for—thank you for everything big and little, I appreciate all that you do, my love has no boundaries and my life is fulfilled with you here.

Roxanne and Louise, two wonderful friends, both qualified chefs and teachers and always there to stimulate and inspire me to reach further and chase my dream— thank you for being there.

Danea, my best friend and soul mate, how lucky I am to have shared many years with this spectacular human being—a kinder, more caring, loving and positive person you will never meet. This book could not have happened without her, juggling family, full-time job and me—it's not easy to have spent literally months pulling together this book with a flow and feel that I am happy to put my name to, and share our life in doing so. Thank you my very, very good friend.

At the helm of Harvest Vegetarian Restaurant is chef, Luke Skilton. Talented and diligent, with an ability to make things happen, Luke is truly a loved and respected young man who contributes daily to the success of our restaurant.

To all my family, friends and fellow food lovers who took the time to help shape this book and remind me always of what a wonderful world it can be, sharing great food with the people we love.

Gather Your Friends,
Create Great Memories,
Feast On Life!

Welcome to the recipes of Harvest Vegetarian Restaurant and the wonderful world of vegetarian cooking.

Vegetarian cooking is my passion and while I am a fully qualified chef and teacher of commercial cookery, as owner and chef of Harvest for the past 14 years, I've gained a great appreciation for the humble 'fruit 'n' veg'.

Harvest began as Beggars Banquet, Sydney's first macrobiotic restaurant, back in the late 1960s; and in 1979 ownership changed and so did the name—to Harvest Vegetarian Restaurant.

Located in the same historic sandstone building in Evans Street, Rozelle, since 1995 we've continued the tradition of fine food, friendly service and creative meals, with a few innovations along the way.

Five years ago I discovered a talented young man, Luke Skilton, who has now completed his apprenticeship at Harvest. Luke is a qualified chef and also the head chef of my restaurant. Often we've been asked for our recipes and at last, here they are, all the favourites plus a few more.

Together we've worked to bring this book to life, so that you can enjoy a life enriched by vegetarian and vegan food.

Whether you're cooking for health, lifestyle or simply looking to add interest to your repertoire, I hope you'll agree that the fresh and tasty recipes here are worthy as meals in their own right.

Fresh from the garden and made with the heart! Try it—your family and friends will thank you for it.

Adam

a walk in the garden

What a wonderful reward it is to walk in the garden and be able to hand-pick the freshest of herbs and produce from your own garden!

Even in my own small courtyard I manage to grow a range of herbs, including basil, lemon thyme and mint, as well as cherry tomatoes and lettuces. Most herbs can be grown in pots, providing for wonderful table or room decorations—they're easy to grow, and it's fun when you're gardening for cooking!

Your garden can be a further source of colourful edible fascination—try marigold petals in a salad or as a substitute for saffron, rose petal water or rose flavoured sugar syrup, nasturtium leaves added into a green salad for extra zing while their flower buds and unripened fruit can be used to replace capers in recipes … not to mention sugared sweet pea flowers and violet-flavoured icing sugar for sweet treats.

Although spices are often a little harder to grow, curry leaves, chillies and peppers can still be grown while others are just more practical to buy—always from a reputable supplier.

A good place to start or add to your own kitchen collection is your local plant nursery—a great place to go and wander around, look at herbs and plan for their mature size in your garden or pots, and perhaps purchase a few seeds or seedlings while you're there.

Simply add water + love + a little organic fertiliser and you're on your way.

polenta mix bread

Preparation Time: 1 hour   Cooking Time: 45 minutes   Makes: 8 small loaves or 4 large loaves   **Vegan**

gather

1¼ kg (5 cups, 2¾ lb) white flour
750g (3 cups, 1.5 lb) wholemeal flour
500g (2 cups, 1.1 lb) coarse polenta
1 teaspoon salt
500ml (2 cups, 17 fl oz) warm water
1 teaspoon castor sugar or honey
40g (1¼ oz) fresh yeast

create

Preheat oven to 200°C (400°F, Gas Mark 6).

Combine the flour, polenta and salt in a medium bowl. Mix the castor sugar/honey with the warm water and then dissolve the yeast into this mix (any sweetener can be used to activate the yeast, even pineapple juice). Combine dry ingredients and yeast mix, adjust with warm water. Set dough aside in a warm place and allow to rise.

When dough has doubled in size, place on a lightly floured board or benchtop. Punch down until flat and the air is expelled. Knead by rolling and folding the mix. Cut the dough into equal sizes, knead each to size and place in lightly oiled tins. Set aside and allow to rise in a warm place for 30–45 minutes.

Bake for 10 minutes and then reduce temperature to 180°C (350°F, Gas Mark 4) for 35 minutes until bread is free from the sides of the tin. Allow to cool slightly before turning out and cooling on cake rack.

feast

Cut loaves and serve warm with main course.

tomato & olive bread

Preparation Time: 1 hour   Cooking Time: 40–45 minutes   Makes: 2 loaves   **Vegan**

gather

5g dried yeast
400ml (1¾ cups, 14 fl oz) warm water
750g (3 cups, 1½ lb) white flour
1½ teaspoons salt
½ tablespoon sugar
50g (1¾ oz) cumin seeds
50g (1¾ oz) caraway seeds
20 black olives, pitted and halved 60g (¼ cup, 2 oz) tomato paste

create

Preheat oven to 200°C (400°F, Gas Mark 6).

Blend yeast in warm water to activate. Sift the flour and salt in a large bowl, add sugar, cumin and caraway seeds and activated yeast. Mix well to form a soft doughy ball, adding a little flour as you go if it feels too sticky. Place in a greased bowl. Cover with plastic film and place in a warm spot to rise for 1 hour; it should nearly double in size.

Turn out onto a floured board and flatten, then stud with olives and spread with tomato paste. Knead again and cut into loaves. Place into greased loaf pans and allow to rise again.

Bake for 10 minutes then reduce temperature to 180°C (350°F, Gas Mark 4) for 30 minutes or until loaf leaves the sides of the tin. Cool slightly in tin before turning out to cool on a rack.

feast

Wonderful bread to serve with a main course or salad.

lavender shortbread

Preparation Time: 30 minutes   Cooking Time: 30 minutes   Makes: 40

gather

250g (1 cup, 8 oz) butter,
slightly softened
70g (5 tablespoons, 2½ oz)
sugar
seeds of 1 vanilla bean,
scraped
300g (1⅓ cups, 10 oz)
plain flour
30g (3 tablespoons, 1 oz)
lavender flowers

create

Preheat oven to 160°C (325°F, Gas Mark 3).

Beat butter, sugar and vanilla seeds until well combined and starting to lighten in colour, but not light and fluffy in texture. Lightly mix in flour using your hands, add lavender flowers and combine into balls. Place on a greased and floured baking tray or tray lined with baking paper. Flatten balls then place in refrigerator for 10–15 minutes.

Bake for 30 minutes or until lightly golden brown. Cook in middle of oven or if more than one tray, rotate during cooking. Allow biscuits to cool completely on tray. Store in an airtight container.

feast

Decoratively place stems of fresh lavender on a plate then place cut shortbread on top.

dips, sauces & dressings

lime & ginger dipping sauce

Preparation Time: 40 minutes   Cooking Time: 30 minutes   Makes: 1 L (8 cups, 64 fl oz)   **Vegan**

gather

zest of 3 limes, finely
diced
1 knob ginger, finely grated
750ml (3 cups, 26 fl oz)
lime juice
2 tablespoons brown sugar
250ml (1 cup, 8 fl oz) apple
juice
2 tablespoons arrowroot,
optional
1 tablespoon water,
optional

create

In a large saucepan, bring lime zest, ginger, lime juice, sugar and apple juice to the boil. Reduce to simmer for half an hour. Turn off heat and allow to cool. If mixture seems too thin, make a paste of 2 tablespoons arrowroot and 1 tablespoon of cold water and stir into the mixture. Bring to the boil to activate the arrowroot, stirring constantly to avoid lumps. Strain through a sieve for a clear jus or leave as is for an enriched sauce.

orange & lime dressing

Preparation Time: 10 minutes   Cooking Time: No cooking   Makes: 1 L (8 cups, 64 fl oz)   **Gluten-free   Vegan**

gather

100ml (3½ fl oz) fresh
orange juice
300ml (1¼ cups, 10 fl oz)
olive oil
½ bunch lemon thyme,
leaves only
salt and pepper
zest of 1 orange, finely
diced

create

Combine all ingredients and whisk or shake to combine.

asian style dipping sauce

Preparation Time: 15 minutes   Cooking Time: No cooking   Serves: 500ml (2 cups, 16 fl oz)   **Gluten-free**   **Vegan**

gather

200ml (7 fl oz) sweet soy sauce
120ml (½ cup, 4 fl oz) sesame oil
100ml (3½ fl oz) sherry vinegar
80ml ($\frac{1}{3}$ cup, 2½ fl oz) olive oil
60ml (¼ cup, 2 fl oz) balsamic vinegar
2 knobs fresh ginger, finely chopped
2 cloves garlic, finely chopped

create

Create by combining all ingredients.

peanut sauce

Preparation Time: 30 minutes   Cooking Time: No cooking   Makes: 600ml (2¼ cups, 20 fl oz)   **Gluten-free**   **Vegan**

gather

1kg (4 cups, 2.2 lb) raw peanuts
500ml (2 cups, 17 fl oz) coconut milk
250g (1 cup, 8 oz) fruit chutney
10ml (2 teaspoons) lemon juice
125ml (½ cup, 4 fl oz) soy sauce
100ml dry sherry
¼ teaspoon Tabasco sauce
4 spring onions
1 teaspoon ground cumin
1 teaspoon curry powder
1 teaspoon ground ginger

create

Combine all ingredients in a food processor until smooth. Heat and serve.

sweet chilli sauce

Preparation Time: 15 minutes   Cooking Time: 15 minutes   Serves: 10   **Gluten-free**   **Vegan**

gather

500g (2 cups, 1.1 lb)
brown sugar
6 small red chillies (halved
lengthways)
250ml (1 cup, 8 fl oz) white
wine vinegar
250ml (1 cup, 8 fl oz)
water

create

Combine all ingredients in a saucepan and boil over medium heat for about 10–15 minutes or until mixture reaches the consistency of syrup. Remove from heat, cool, serve with Thai Spring Rolls (see page 47) or Vietnamese Rice Paper Rolls (see page 39).

vinaigrette

Preparation Time: 5 minutes   Cooking Time: No cooking   Serves: Variable   **Gluten-free**   **Vegan**

gather

3 parts olive oil
1 part balsamic vinegar
30ml (6 teaspoons, 1 fl oz)
lemon juice
salt and pepper

create

Combine all the ingredients and shake well. This a temporary emulsion which will separate when left to stand, so always shake well before use.

tomato & rosemary jam

Preparation Time: 15 minutes   Cooking Time: 1 hour   Makes: 1kg (4 cups, 2lb)   **Gluten-free**   **Vegan**

gather

1½kg (6 cups, 3.3 lb) ox heart tomatoes, seeded and peeled
1½kg (6 cups, 3.3 lb) castor sugar
juice of 3 lemons
6 sprigs fresh rosemary

Harvest Hint

You can use any type of ripe tomato but my preference is ox heart tomatoes. They are expensive and often hard to obtain but worth it.

create

Seed and peel tomatoes. Roughly chop tomato flesh. Place tomato, sugar, lemon juice and rosemary into a large heavy-based saucepan. Bring to the boil and allow to simmer for 1 hour, or until mixture becomes jelly-like. Remove rosemary sprigs. Pour into warm sterilised jars. Cool before sealing and labelling.
Makes 3–4 jars. Stores for up to three months.

chilli jam

Preparation Time: 15 minutes   Cooking Time: 1–1½ hours   Makes: 500ml (2 cups, 16 fl oz)   **Gluten-free**   **Vegan**

gather

2 spanish onions, diced
8 chillies, sliced
2 red capsicums, roasted, peeled and seeded
250ml (1 cup, 8 fl oz) water
1 teaspoon cumin
1kg (4 cups, 2.2 lb) castor sugar
20ml (1 tablespoon, ½ fl oz) vinegar, if needed

create

Place onions and chillies in a large frying pan. Add roasted capsicum. Add water then cumin. Bring to the boil and reduce heat. Add all sugar, covering all the mix in the pan. Allow to simmer for 1–1½ hours. Test jam consistency by placing a teaspoon of mix in the refrigerator to cool. If too thick, adjust consistency by adding vinegar, if too thin, return to heat and allow to thicken, stirring occasionally. Pour into warm sterilised jars. Cool before sealing and labelling. Makes 3 jars. Stores for up to three months.

avocado salsa

Preparation Time: 30 minutes   Cooking Time: No cooking   Makes: 1½kg (6 cups, 3lb)   **Gluten-free   Vegan**

gather

Salsa
2 avocados, large, flesh
chopped
1 medium spanish onion, finely
diced
1 tablespoon (½ fl oz) lime juice
1 medium roma or egg tomato,
peeled, seeded
1 small red capsicum, roasted
and skins removed
1 teaspoon ground coriander
(cilantro)
1 teaspoon ground cumin
3 tablespoons fresh mint
leaves, chopped
2 fresh chillies
30ml (6 teaspoons, 1 fl oz)
olive oil
4–5 drops Tabasco sauce

Dressing
30ml (1 fl oz) lime juice
90ml (3 fl oz) olive oil
¼ teaspoon ground cumin
½ bunch coriander (cilantro)
leaves, finely sliced
½ bunch mint leaves, finely cut
1 teaspoon Tabasco sauce
1 red capsicum, finely diced
corn chips to serve

create

Cut the avocados in half, scoop out flesh with
a serving spoon and finely chop. Place avocado flesh
and diced onion in a medium bowl and toss lightly with
lime juice. Retain the shells for serving.

Dice tomato and cut capsicum flesh into strips and set
aside. Place the ground coriander and cumin in a small
pan; stir over medium heat for 1 minute to enhance
fragrance and flavour, remove from heat and allow
to cool.

Add all salsa ingredients to the avocado and onion mix
and gently combine so that the avocado retains its
shape and is not mashed. Refrigerate until required.

Combine the dressing ingredients and shake well.
Refrigerate until required.

Allow salsa to come to room temperature before
serving in avocado shells or placed on an inverted shell
on a plate, using it as a platform for the salsa piled
decoratively on top.

feast

Drizzle with dressing and accompany with corn
chips.

rocket pesto

Preparation Time: 30 minutes   Cooking Time: No cooking   Makes: 250g (1 cup, 8 oz)   **Gluten-free**

gather

2 bunches of rocket
(arugula)
250g (1 cup, 8 oz) pine
nuts, lightly roasted if
desired
2 to 3 cloves garlic
80g (7 tablespoons, 3 oz)
fresh parmesan cheese
10ml (2 teaspoons) oil
squeeze of lemon juice
250–500ml (1–2 cups,
8–16 fl oz cream) optional

create

Whiz all the ingredients in a food processor to a smooth paste. Add salt and pepper to taste. If using as a sauce, add 1 or 2 cups of cream over heat and allow to thicken.

fresh tomato salsa

Preparation Time: 30 minutes   Cooking Time: No cooking   Serves: 4   **Gluten-free**   **Vegan**

gather

6 egg tomatoes or 2 large
tomatoes, firmly ripe
5g salad onion or green
shallot, very finely chopped
2 teaspoons fresh lemon
or lime juice
2 teaspoons olive oil
a few drops balsamic
vinegar (optional)
chopped fresh herbs to
taste (use basil, coriander
(cilantro), parsley or mint)
dash Tabasco or mild
sweet chilli sauce

create

The tomatoes can be peeled or not as you wish—cut into halves then gently squeeze away the seeds. Cut the tomato flesh into small dice and put it into a small bowl, then add the remaining ingredients and season to taste with salt and pepper. Cover and leave at room temperature for about 30 minutes for the flavours to infuse.

classic sauces
hollandaise sauce

Preparation Time: 30 minutes   Cooking Time: 15 minutes   Makes: 200ml (6½ fl oz)   **Gluten-free**

gather

60ml (¼ cup, 2 fl oz) white wine vinegar
6 peppercorns
1 bay leaf (exclude in blender method)
3 egg yolks
125g (½ cup, 4 oz) unsalted butter, chopped into pieces
5ml (1 teaspoon) lemon juice
salt and pepper

create

Traditional Method

Simmer white wine vinegar, 6 peppercorns and bay leaf until reduced to 30ml (6 teaspoons, 1 fl oz). Strain and cool slightly. Combine reduced vinegar and egg yolks in the top of a double saucepan and whisk continuously over a gentle heat until creamy and slightly thickened. Continue whisking while adding unsalted butter—a small piece at a time. When all the butter has been added, remove from heat and whisk in lemon juice and salt and pepper to taste. Adjust with extra vinegar if you prefer a sharper taste.

Blender Method

Melt butter in the microwave for 2 minutes on high. Beat egg yolks, 10ml (2 teaspoons, $^2/_5$ fl oz) lemon juice and freshly ground black pepper in a blender. Gradually add 'bubbly hot' melted butter while blender is operating. Add vinegar at the end, taste and adjust.

feast

A treat for any vegetable mix, ladled over asparagus, or a topping for poached eggs or salads.

mayonnaise

Preparation Time: 10 minutes   Cooking Time: No cooking   Makes: 250g (1 cup, 8 oz)   **Gluten-free**

gather

3 egg yolks
1 whole egg
200ml (7 fl oz) olive oil
salt and pepper

create

Beat eggs until pale cream in colour. Leave machine on high and slowly pour in the olive oil, one-quarter at a time, allowing it to thicken before adding more. Continue until all the oil is well incorporated. Season with salt and pepper to taste. Note that the quality of your oil will determine the quality of your mayonnaise.

béarnaise sauce

Preparation Time: 30 minutes   Cooking Time: 15 minutes Makes: 200ml (6½ fl oz)   **Gluten-free**

gather

60ml (¼ cup, 2 fl oz) tarragon vinegar
6 peppercorns
1 bay leaf
2 egg yolks
125g (½ cup, 4 oz) unsalted butter, chopped into pieces
5ml (1 teaspoon) lemon juice
1 bunch tarragon, finely chopped
salt and pepper

create

Simmer tarragon vinegar, peppercorns and bay leaf until reduced to 30ml (6 teaspoons, 1fl oz). Strain and cool slightly. Combine reduced vinegar and egg yolks in the top of a double saucepan and whisk continuously over a gentle heat until creamy and slightly thickened. Continue whisking while adding unsalted butter—a small piece at a time. When all the butter has been added, remove from heat and whisk in lemon juice, tarragon and salt and pepper to taste. Adjust with extra vinegar if you prefer a sharper taste.

tapas plate

lentil, mint & lemon dip

Gluten-free   Vegan

gather

100g (½ cup, 3½ oz) puy lentils
300ml (1¼ cups, 10 fl oz) water
1 teaspoon cumin seeds, toasted and crushed
1 garlic clove, crushed
4 tablespoons mint, finely chopped
3 tablespoons lemon juice
3 tablespoons olive oil
zest of 1 lemon
salt and pepper

create

Put lentils in a saucepan with water. Bring to the boil and simmer for 5 minutes until soft, then drain. Put the lentils in a food processor with the remaining ingredients and process until smooth. Add more lemon juice as preferred, and salt and pepper to taste if necessary.

fetta & oregano dip

Gluten-free

gather

500g (1.1 lb) greek fetta, crumbled
50g (1¾ oz) rich blue vein cheese, crumbled
60ml (¼ cup, 2 fl oz) natural greek yoghurt
60ml (¼ cup, 2 fl oz) olive oil
2 teaspoons oregano, chopped
2 fresh, small red chillies, chopped

create

Combine cheeses, yoghurt, oil, oregano and chilli in a bowl and mix well. Pour into a jar, then add a film of olive oil over it to seal. Serve garnished with oregano and chilli.

guacamole

Gluten-free   Vegan

gather

2 to 3 avocados
1 clove garlic, crushed
juice of half a lemon
40ml (2 tablespoons,
1$^3/_5$ fl oz) olive oil
salt and pepper

create

Process avocado flesh until smooth, add all other ingredients and process for 1 minute more.

mushroom ragout

Gluten-free   Vegan

gather

1kg (4 cups, 2.2 lb) button
mushrooms, finely diced
3 cloves garlic
oil for frying
salt and pepper
6 yellow or green zucchinis
(courgettes), diced
6 spanish onions, diced
500g (2 cups, 1.1 lb)
tomato puree
250g (1 cup, 8 oz) mixed
herbs (rosemary, sage,
mint, thyme, basil), finely
diced
salt and pepper

create

Sauté mushrooms with garlic, salt and pepper until brown—remove and drain liquid.

Fry onions and zucchini flesh until brown, add herbs and stir well. Add tomato puree
and bring to a gentle simmer. Remove from heat and fold in sautéed mushrooms. Season with salt and pepper.

feast

Four great dips—serve a spoonful of each on individual plates or use colourful bowls for easy entertaining. Accompy them with your choice of favourite toasted breads or corn chips.

zucchini flowers filled with fetta, ricotta & herbs

Preparation Time: 30 minutes   Cooking Time: 20–30 minutes   Serves: 4–6   **Gluten-free**

gather

1 red capsicum, large, roasted and skins removed
2 spring onions, diced finely
100g (½ cup, 3½ oz) fetta cheese, crumbled
200g (7 oz) ricotta cheese, crumbled
1 clove garlic, crushed
1 tablespoon oregano, finely chopped
1 tablespoon sage, finely chopped
salt and pepper
12 zucchini flowers

olive oil if deep drying

Harvest Hint
A 'bain-marie' is a water bath used for gentler indirect cooking. It is commonly a tray floating within a tray filled with warm water one-quarter to halfway up the side of the tray. It is covered with foil to create a steam oven.

create

Preheat oven to 180°C (350°F, Gas Mark 4).

Finely dice capsicum flesh. Lightly fry onions and remove from heat. Combine with remaining ingredients except zucchini flowers.

Trim stems from the flowers (if you find a small zucchini growing on the end, don't cut it off or throw it away—these are edible and delicious). Spoon mixture into the centre of the flowers. Twist and fold petals to secure.

Place on a tray lined with baking paper in a bain-marie filled with water one-quarter up the side of the bath.

Bake until soft, about 20–30 minutes. Serve warm.

The flowers can also be battered or crumbed and deep-fried, drain well before serving.

feast

Serve with a side salad of rocket and include a few fresh nasturtium flowers.

stuffed capsicums

Preparation Time: 1 hour   Cooking Time: 1 hour   Serves: 6   **Gluten-free Vegan**

6 large capsicums (sweet peppers)
1kg (4 cups, 2.2 lb) short grain white rice
2 carrots, shredded
1 teaspoon cumin
2 large onions, finely diced
1 vegetable stock cube
6 tomatoes, hulled, flesh retained, then diced
1 eggplant, peeled and flesh diced
250g (1 cup, 8 oz) mushrooms (optional)
½ bunch parsley
salt and pepper
250ml (1 cup, 10 fl oz) olive oil

Preheat oven to 180°C (350°F, Gas Mark 4).

To prepare capsicums, cut root end off and retain as a lid for the stuffed capsicums. Hull the capsicums and discard membrane and seeds.

Combine all the ingredients, ensuring that your mixture is moist throughout or add extra oil as required. Add salt and pepper to taste.

Fill capsicums three-quarters full with mixture to allow room for rice to expand. Drizzle olive oil on top of mix then place lid on top. Place capsicums upright, uncovered, in a cake tin or baking tray.

Bake for up to 1 hour until tender and roasted.

Serve hot or cold and add a dollop of rosemary jam.

food
on the go

Life is so hurried these days and it seems that we're always on the move and often away from home. Satisfying our appetite when we're away from home can be so expensive, quality can be questionable and dietary requirements not always available—so why not spend a bit of time planning ahead to help make life a little less hectic while still enjoying the food you want.

This chapter contains recipes that are ideal for work lunches, taking on picnics, or freezing portions for those evenings when you don't feel like cooking—essentially those recipes that I'd refer to as food on the go.

stuffed mushrooms

gather

500g (1.1 lb) medium-sized mushrooms

Filling
50g (1¾ oz) spring onions
50g (1¾ oz) celery
1 clove garlic, crushed or finely chopped
3–4 sprigs (1 tablespoon) sage, finely chopped
60g (¼ cup, 2 oz) roasted tomato puree
salt and pepper

Crumbing Mix
100g (½ cup, 3½ oz) plain flour, seasoned
2 eggs
30ml (6 teaspoons, 1 fl oz) milk
100g (½ cup, 3½ oz) polenta
200g (8 oz) fresh breadcrumbs

oil for frying

create

Remove stalks from 4–6 mushrooms and hull out flesh, retaining it for the filling. Be careful not to break through the mushroom casings. Cover and set aside in refrigerator.

To make the filling, dice onions, celery and garlic. Pan-fry onions until golden, add garlic, sage and celery, stir for 1 minute and remove from pan, set aside. Cut remaining mushrooms and add to pan with previously retained mushroom flesh. Add salt and pepper and pan-fry until soft and reduced. Add roasted tomato puree (or tomato paste). Remove from heat and combine with onion mix. Drain any excess liquid. Add some breadcrumbs to absorb retained moisture. Remove mushroom casings from refrigerator and fill with mushroom mix.

Gather your crumbing ingredients and set out in 3 bowls—flour and seasoning, lightly beaten eggs with milk, and polenta and breadcrumbs (fresh breadcrumbs for colouring is preferred).

Take each mushroom and roll first in flour, dust off excess and dip in egg-wash. Let excess drip off and then roll in crumbing mix. Repeat egg and breadcrumb steps (not flour). Deep-fry or shallow-fry for 7–10 minutes, turning if necessary to ensure even cooking.

feast

A great party stopper, entrée or extra for any meal.

nutty leek & cheese tart

Preparation Time: 45 minutes   Cooking Time: 1 hour   Serves: 8

gather

300g (10 oz) puff pastry

Filling

2 leeks, centres only, finely sliced
15g (½ oz) butter
40ml (2 tablespoons, 1³/₅ fl oz) olive oil
1 teaspoon fresh lemon thyme leaves
freshly ground pepper
50g (1¾ oz) walnuts, chopped coarsely
60g (¼ cup, 2 oz) parmesan cheese, grated
60g (¼ cup, 2 oz) mozzarella cheese, grated
60g (¼ cup, 2 oz) gruyere cheese, crumbled
60g (¼ cup, 2 oz) fetta cheese
2 eggs, beaten

create

Preheat oven to 190°C (375°F, Gas Mark 5).

Roll out pastry on a floured surface to a thickness of 2 to 3cm (about an inch). Cut to suit your pastry tin (large or individual tins, which should be greased and floured). Line tin with pastry, prick evenly and bake blind until just golden.

Heat butter and and oil and fry leeks, then add lemon thyme and black pepper. Add walnuts and cook until they look roasted. Allow to cool.

Add cheeses and beaten eggs, then combine with mix. Fill pastry tarts and bake for 30–40 minutes or until brown.

Harvest Hint

Baking blind is often used to create a crisp, cooked pastry shell before adding the filling. Grease and flour pastry tin as usual and line with pastry, prick pastry evenly with a fork. Place a sheet of baking paper on top, top with dry rice or store bought baking beans. Bake for 20–30 minutes, remove the paper and rice and proceed with the recipe.

feast

A rich tasty tart, beautiful served with a fresh green salad.

vietnamese rice paper rolls

Preparation Time: 15 minutes   Cooking Time: 20–30 minutes   Serves: 40   **Gluten-free**   **Vegan**

gather

1 firm block (450g, 14½ oz) tofu (marinade optional)

vegetable oil for deep-frying

1 bunch english or baby spinach (raw, washed, chopped and washed again)

3 carrots (shredded through food processor or grated)

3 spring onions (shredded or finely chopped)

2 bunches fresh mint leaves, chopped

1 packet rice paper sheets

200ml (7 fl oz) soy sauce (optional marinade, add 1 hour to preparation time)

30ml (6 teaspoons, 1 fl oz) lemon juice (include in marinade)

create

Cut tofu into small cubes. If marinating for extra flavour, cover cubes with soy sauce and lemon juice for up to an hour. Deep-fry tofu cubes in hot oil until golden.

Ensure excess liquid has been drained from the freshly shredded ingredients (e.g. carrots, as too much moisture can make for a sloppy mix) then combine all ingredients with tofu and seal in an airtight container until ready to assemble.

To assemble rolls, soak three sheets of rice paper at a time in warm water for 1 minute, then remove and place on a clean towel. Pat dry and allow to stand for 1 minute.

Place a small quantity of mix on rice paper and roll into a cylinder, tucking in side edges as you roll. Place on a tray and cover with plastic wrap, store in refrigerator.

The finished rolls are served cold and cut in half diagonally, with three or four pieces standing together on the plate to create a visually appealing dish. Garnish with mint or coriander leaves and accompany with Sweet Chilli Sauce (see page 19).

feast

An easy recipe to prepare ahead and take for lunches or picnics. The filling will store for up to two days, sealed and refrigerated. Any combination of ingredients can be used for the filling.

potato & corn rosti

Preparation Time: 15 minutes   Cooking Time: 10 minutes   Serves: 12

gather

750g (3 cups, 1.5 lb) pontiac potatoes, peeled and shredded
1 spring onion, grated
4 cobs of corn, cooked
375g (1½ cups, 12 oz) plain flour
2 tablespoons salt and lemon pepper
2 eggs, lightly beaten
1 bunch lemon thyme, leaves only
vegetable oil for shallow frying

create

Place potatoes and onion in a large sieve and squeeze out excess liquid (starch). Cut corn kernels off cob and add to potato mix.

Combine flour, salt and pepper separately, then mix into potato and corn mix. Add beaten eggs. Next add lemon thyme leaves and stir through.

The mix should pull together to shape into patties. Shallow-fry till lightly brown, then pat dry and place on absorbent paper to remove excess oil before serving.

feast

Rosti can also be reheated by deep-frying, or served cold for a picnic, lunch or party food. Serve with a yoghurt and dill mix if wanted.

steamed spicy vegetarian buns

Preparation Time: 40 minutes   Cooking Time: 10 minutes   Serves: 6   **Vegan**

gather

Dough

10g (¹⁄₃ oz) fresh yeast

125ml (½ cup, 4 fl oz) warm water

60g (¼ cup, 2 oz) honey

250g (1 cup, 8 oz) plain flour

Filling

3 roman brown mushrooms, chopped

50g (1¾ oz) marinated tofu

½ leek, finely chopped

2 cloves garlic, crushed

1 teaspoon ginger, grated

250g (1 cup, 8 oz) unsalted cashews, roasted

½ teaspoon anise

1 tablespoon mint, freshly chopped

10ml (2 teaspoons) Sweet Chilli Sauce (optional)

30g (1 oz) pine nuts

vegetable oil for pan-frying

sesame oil for steamer

create

Form the dough by combining yeast, warm water and honey and mixing together with a fork. Place in warm spot (e.g. on oven top). When foam appears on top, the yeast is activated. Add to flour to make a dough. Knead on a floured board until tight and springy.

To make the filling, fry the chopped mushrooms, leek, garlic, tofu and ginger in a pan. Remove from heat and add cashews, anise and mint, and Sweet Chilli Sauce if using. Fold in pine nuts and place to one side.

Cut dough into 6–12 even pieces. Roll out each piece to form a circle.

Place a tablespoon of filling into centre of each circle, gather edges and roll into a ball.

Brush greaseproof paper with sesame oil and place in steamer with buns on top for 8 minutes or until dry to touch.

feast

Serve with Sweet Chilli Sauce (see page 19).

almond & leek soup

Preparation Time: 20 minutes   Cooking Time: 20 minutes   Serves: 8

gather

1 L (8 cups, 64 fl oz) milk
500ml (2 cups, 16 fl oz) cream
500ml (2 cups, 16 fl oz) vegetable stock
1 leek, finely sliced
½ celery, finely cut
250g (1 cup, 8 oz) blanched almonds, ground
pinch nutmeg
125g (½ cup, 4 oz) butter
125g (½ cup, 4 oz) flour
125g (½ cup, 4 oz) slivered almonds, toasted for garnish
salt and pepper to taste

create

In a pot, place milk, cream, vegetable stock, leek, celery, nutmeg and ground almonds and simmer.

Melt butter, then add all flour and cook for 2 minutes over medium heat.

Add milk mixture to the flour roux and stir until thick.

Season and adjust consistency with a little milk if required.

feast

Garnish with toasted almonds.
Delicious served hot or cold!

zucchini, tomato & roasted capsicum terrine

Preparation Time: 45 minutes   Cooking Time: 1 hour   Serves: 8–10   **Gluten-free Vegan**

gather

4 capsicums (sweet peppers), roasted and skins removed
5 zucchinis (courgettes), sliced thinly into strips
a little olive oil
4 teaspoons ground cumin
salt and freshly ground pepper
1 medium onion, finely diced
2 cloves garlic, crushed and diced
1 kg (4 cups, 2.2 lb) ripe roma tomatoes, peeled, seeded and diced
1 bunch basil
150g (5 oz) sun-dried tomatoes, sliced thinly

create

Cut capsicum flesh into wide strips.

Brush zucchini slices with olive oil and sprinkle with cumin. Grill on both sides until lightly brown. Sprinkle with salt and pepper. Set aside to cool.

Sauté onion and garlic in olive oil until translucent (not coloured). Add diced tomatoes and 3 chopped basil leaves (set aside remainder of basil leaves). Cook for 5 minutes, remove from heat and set aside.

Line a terrine dish with plastic film. Start with a layer of zucchini slices, then cover completely with a layer of basil leaves.

Next cover with tomato mixture then a layer of sun-dried tomatoes, then capsicum strips. Repeat all layers until the terrine dish is full.

Cover with plastic film and place weights on top. Refrigerate for several hours or overnight before turning out. Cut into slices to serve.

Harvest Hint

To easily roast and peel capsicums, cut in half, then discard seeds and membrane. Brush skin with oil and place oil side up on tray under high grill until skin is blackened. Remove and place in plastic bag in refrigerator while hot for 10 minutes. This will sweat the skin loose.

feast

Delicious served with toasted pita bread or french bread. Keeps well in the refrigerator.

thai spring rolls

Preparation Time: 30–45 minutes   Cooking Time: 5–6 minutes   Serves: 20   **Vegan**

gather

40ml (2 tablespoons,
1³/₅ fl oz) sesame oil
40ml (2 tablespoons,
1³/₅ fl oz) vegetable oil
3 spanish onions, peeled
and chopped
4 cloves garlic, peeled and
finely chopped
70g (2½ oz) ginger, peeled
and finely chopped
1 bunch coriander
(cilantro), roots and leaves
chopped separately
3 bok choy, finely sliced
3 carrots, peeled and
julienned
100ml (3½ fl oz) sweet soy
sauce
1 red capsicum (sweet
pepper), roasted, skins
removed and diced

1 packet spring roll
wrappers

flour and water to seal rolls
vegetable oil for
deep-frying

create

In a heavy saucepan, heat sesame and vegetable oils, add onions and garlic and fry lightly until soft. Add ginger, coriander roots and bok choy and cook over medium heat for a few minutes—then add carrots. Cook for a couple of minutes more, stirring constantly. Add soy sauce, diced capsicum and chopped coriander leaves. Remove from heat and place vegetables in a colander to drain any excess oil.

To assemble the rolls, take a spring roll wrapper and place it with a corner facing you. Place 2 tablespoons of filling in the corner of the wrapper and start rolling, folding in the sides as you go. The aim is to make a firm and unbroken roll. Seal end with a little flour/water mix. Repeat with remaining filling and wrappers.

Deep-fry in hot oil, cook until golden and drain well on absorbent paper. Serve with Sweet Chilli Sauce (see page 19) or your favourite dipping sauce.

Harvest Hint
The term 'julienne' means to finely cut vegetables into matchstick sized pieces.

feast

Can be frozen for up to three months, but they must be deep-fried while still frozen, do not thaw them before cooking.

potato & olive cake

Preparation Time: 30 minutes   Cooking Time: 30 minutes   Serves: 4–6

gather

2kg (8 cups, 4.4 lb) pontiac potatoes, peeled and roughly chopped
3 cloves garlic, finely diced
2 tablespoons ground cumin
20g butter
50g (1¾ oz) gruyere cheese
2 eggs, lightly beaten
salt and pepper
500g (2 cups, 1.1 lb) fresh breadcrumbs
1 quantity Rocket Pesto (see page 22)
10 pitted kalamata olives
50g (1¾ oz) fetta cheese, diced
50g (1¾ oz) parmesan cheese, grated

250–500ml (1–2 cups, 8–16 fl oz) cream
3 tablespoons Rocket Pesto

create

Preheat oven to 200°C (400°F, Gas Mark 6).

Boil potatoes and drain well, then mash with garlic, cumin and butter. Fold gruyere cheese through and add lightly beaten eggs. Add salt and pepper to taste.

Grease a pie tin and coat with a thick layer of breadcrumbs. Add a layer of potato mix then top with a thin layer of pesto. Insert 5 olives and sprinkle with gruyere, then insert 6 squares of fetta. Repeat layers of potato, pesto, olives and fetta then sprinkle lightly with parmesan.

Bake for 30 minutes or until golden.

Serve with a pesto cream sauce, made by combining cream and pesto over heat and allowing it to thicken, stirring frequently.

feast

Accompany with a greek salad or rocket and mesclun salad with red and yellow tear tomatoes.

vegetarian coming to dinner

'Oh no!' Many people are attracted to the idea of vegetarian food but fear the thought of bland meals with a lack of flavour and substance. This leaves people with a conundrum as to what to do, but fear no more.

These recipes are easy to prepare and will suit 'meat eaters' and 'vegetarians' alike, even vegans can be catered for without sending you into a frenzy of indecision.

Everybody will love these recipes—no longer do you need to cook separate meals just because a vegetarian is coming to dinner!

fetta parcels

Preparation Time: 30 minutes   Cooking Time: 30 minutes   Serves: 4

gather

250g (1 cup, 8 oz) unsalted butter
500g (1 lb) fetta cheese
50g (1¾ oz) pesto
1 packet filo pastry
2 tablespoons sesame seeds

create

Preheat oven to 200°C (400°F, Gas Mark 6).

Clarify butter by gently heating in a saucepan until melted and the milk solids have separated from the butter fat. Allow to cool, drain off the butter fat component and set aside. Discard the milk solids that sink to the bottom.

Cut fetta into 2–3cm (about 1 inch) blocks (8 pieces). Place a teaspoon of pesto on top of each block.

Cut filo pastry into pieces 12cm wide by 30cm long (5 by 12 inches), 16 pieces in total.

Lay pastry pieces in a stack on the bench and place one block of fetta with pesto on it.

Lightly brush the exposed surface of pastry with clarified butter and fold the fetta to form a parcel.

Repeat for a second layer, brushing the parcel again with butter then sprinkling with sesame seeds.

Repeat for remaining parcels.

Place parcels on a baking tray and bake in a preheated oven for 20–30 minutes.

feast

Serve with fresh garden salad or as a tasty treat on their own.
They can also be frozen then cooked later.

mouth-watering moussaka

Preparation Time: 90 minutes   Cooking Time: 2 hours   Serves: 12

gather

Salsa

20ml (1 tablespoon, ½ fl oz) oil
2 onions, finely chopped
2 large carrots, peeled and
finely chopped
250g (1 cup, 8 oz) mushrooms,
roughly chopped
½ bunch parsley, finely chopped
salt and pepper
750g (3 cups, 1.5 lb) roasted
tomatoes, chopped
½ eggplant, diced
250g (1 cup, 8 oz) tomato paste
breadcrumbs (enough to cover
base of dish you are using)

Layers

3 large eggplants, sliced
lengthways about 1cm thick
10 large potatoes, peeled and
sliced about 1cm (½ inch) thick
750g (3 cups, 1.5 lb) parmesan
cheese, grated

White Sauce

100g (½ cup, 3½ oz) cornflour
1.75 L (7 cups, 3¾ pints) milk

Preheat oven to 180°C (350°F, Gas Mark 4).

For the salsa, heat oil in a large frypan and fry onions until transparent. Add carrots, mushrooms and parsley, salt and pepper to taste and reduce heat. Add the chopped tomatoes and diced eggplant, then stir in the tomato paste. Leave to cook, checking often, for about an hour on low heat. Set aside when cooked.

Salt the potato slices and place in a large baking tray, coat with a light oil. Cover with foil and bake for about an hour. (Do not overcook as you won't be able to work with them.)

Totally cover sliced eggplants with salt and let stand for 15 minutes. Then immerse them in water for a further 15 minutes. When done gently squeeze all the water out of the eggplants, being careful not to break them. Coat slices with oil, place in a baking tray covered with foil and bake for an hour. (Once again, do not overcook for ease of handling.)

To assemble the moussaka, using a large deep baking tray, layer and spread one ladle of salsa over base, then sprinkle with a light layer of breadcrumbs. (This stops the dish from sticking at the bottom of the tray.)

Lay one row of potato slices, top with one layer of eggplants, top with half the batch of sauce and sprinkle with half the parmesan. Repeat this process for a second layer.

To make white sauce, bring three-quarters of the milk to the boil and reduce heat to a simmer. Make a paste from the remainder of the milk and the cornflour and mix into the hot milk. Whisk until thick, simmer for 1 minute, stirring constantly. Spread the sauce over the dish carefully and top with parmesan. Bake until golden brown, 30–40 minutes approximately.

Serve with fresh garden salad or as a tasty treat on its own.

tofu skewers & peanut sauce

Preparation Time: 30 minutes   Cooking Time: 1 hour   Serves: 4   **Gluten-free Vegan**

Peanut Sauce
(see page 18)

gather

1 red capsicum
1 kumara, peeled
1 potato, peeled
1 turnip, peeled
oil
salt and pepper
1 spanish onion, cut into
quarters
1 firm block (450g, 14½ oz)
tofu, marinated if preferred

create

Preheat oven to 180°C (350°F, Gas Mark 4).

Roast capsicum flesh and cut into bite-sized squares.

Cut root vegetables into bite-sized chunks, brush with oil and season with salt and pepper. Roast until tender in a hot oven, about 45 minutes.

Cut spanish onion into quarters and pan-fry for colour.

Cut tofu into bite-sized cubes (marinate beforehand in your favourite soy sauce if preferred) and bake (30–45 minutes) or deep-fry until golden.

Assemble ingredients on skewers, beginning and ending with a tofu cube and alternating vegetables in between.

Heat in oven before serving with Peanut Sauce.

feast

A good dish to make ahead of time and then reheat.

risotto cakes with roasted red pepper sauce

Preparation Time: 1 hour Cooking Time: 1 hour Serves: 8 **Gluten-free Vegan**

gather

10 red capsicums (sweet peppers)
750g (3 cups, 1.5 lb) tomato puree (about 6–8 tomatoes)
1 spanish onion, finely chopped
3 cloves garlic, chopped
2 bunches tarragon, leaves only
200ml (7 fl oz) dry white wine
250g (1 cup, 8 oz) arborio rice
1 L (4 cups, 34 fl oz) vegetable stock
2 bunches english spinach, trimmed and washed
olive oil

create

De-seed then roast red capsicum until black, remove skin then puree for the sauce.

Roast and puree tomatoes, add to capsicum puree.

Fry spanish onion until light brown, add chopped garlic and half the tarragon. Add white wine, then reduce. Stir in rice, then add stock and stir constantly until cooked.

Cut spinach into shreds and add to risotto mix with remaining tarragon.

Shape or mould mix in a cup or bowl and invert on a plate.

feast

Serve with roasted pepper and tomato sauce.

coconut curry

Preparation Time: 30 minutes   Cooking Time: 30 minutes Serves: 4–6   **Gluten-free   Vegan**

gather

oil for frying
3–4 spanish onions
3 chillies, finely chopped
1 tablespoon garlic
8 curry leaves
salt and pepper
½ teaspoon turmeric
½ teaspoon cumin
½ teaspoon garam masala
1 teaspoon curry powder
½ teaspoon paprika
600ml (2½ cups, 20 fl oz)
coconut milk
1 teaspoon tamarind
2 potatoes, roasted and
chopped into small cubes
1 sweet potato, roasted and
chopped into small cubes
¼ cauliflower, chopped into
small florets and blanched
100g (½ cup, 3½ oz) snow
peas, blanched
200g (7 oz) green beans, cut
into bite-sized pieces and
blanched
1 carrot, sliced and blanched

create

Heat oil and fry onions until light golden brown. Add chillies then the garlic and curry leaves. Add salt and pepper to taste and reduce heat.

Dry-fry combined spices then add to onion mix. Cook on low heat for 2–3 minutes.

Add coconut milk 1 cup at a time, stirring in between. Add tamarind and simmer for 20–30 minutes to thicken the curry mix.

Before serving, add roasted potatoes and cauliflower to curry mix and heat through, stirring gently, for about 2–3 minutes. Just before serving, add snow peas, green beans and carrots and mix through.

feast

A great dish on its own or accompanied with basmati rice, pappadums, fruit chutney and banana sambal.

kumera & english spinach gnocchi

Preparation Time: 30 minutes   Cooking Time: 30 minutes   Serves: 6   **Vegan**

gather

500g (2 cups, 1.1 lb) desiree or pontiac potatoes, peeled and roughly chopped

250g (1 cup, 8 oz) kumara (sweet potato), peeled and roughly chopped

2 tablespoons salt

pepper to taste

1 bunch lemon thyme, leaves only

90g (3 oz) english spinach leaves (wash, chop and wash again)

2 tablespoons fresh basil or oregano, finely chopped

500g (2 cups, 1.1 lb) plain flour

Sauce (not included in vegan option)

300ml (1¼ cups, 10 fl oz) cream

2 cloves garlic, crushed

juice of 1 lemon

250g (1 cup, 8 oz) parmesan, grated

create

Boil potatoes until just cooked—when a wooden skewer can just be inserted, do not overcook. Drain. When cool, peel and return to pan to dry off well. Mash until smooth.

Boil kumara until just cooked. (Do not cook with potatoes as each has a different cooking time.) Drain and mash.

Combine potato and kumara mash, salt, pepper to taste, lemon thyme leaves, chopped spinach and basil or oregano. Add flour to thicken and mix thoroughly.

Wash and oil your hands and roll a teaspoon of gnocchi mix into a ball. Place on a tray and continue until all the mix is rolled. You will need to wash and oil your hands as you go.

Roll each ball in the seasoned flour and roll in clean, floured hands for up to two minutes each, to help develop the gluten and allows the gnocchi balls to maintain their shape when cooking. Place balls on a clean tray and continue until all the gnocchi is rolled and ready to cook.

Drop 6–8 balls at a time into a saucepan of lightly salted boiling water. They rise to the top when cooked. Remove and place in sauce. (Or, prior to placing in sauce, you can keep in refrigerator for two days or freeze for later use.)

Combine cream, garlic and lemon juice in a saucepan—bring all ingredients to the boil then simmer until thick. Stir frequently. Place gnocchi in sauce and stir to coat. Transfer into an ovenproof serving dish and cover with grated parmesan then grill until golden.

split pea coconut soup

Preparation Time: 24 hours   Cooking Time: 1 hour   Serves: 10   **Gluten-free Vegan**

gather

4 spanish onions, diced

2 cloves garlic

3 teaspoons cumin

2 teaspoons fresh ginger, finely diced

2 teaspoons turmeric

2 bunches coriander (cilantro)

500g (1 lb) split green peas (soaked for 24 hours, changing water twice)

700ml (2 x 350ml tins/ 24 fl oz) coconut milk

salt and pepper

create

Sauté onions and garlic, add spices. Add peas and coconut milk.

Add enough water to cover by 5cm (2 inches), bring to the boil then simmer for 30–45 minutes.

Blend and adjust seasoning to taste.

feast

Grind fresh pepper over the top to serve and add a sprig of coriander.

sweet & sour tofu

Preparation Time: 45 minutes   Cooking Time: 30 minutes   Serves: 4

gather

1 firm block (450g, 14½ oz) tofu
60g (¼ cup, 2 oz) flour
1 egg, beaten
165g (5½ oz) capsicums (sweet peppers), red and green
80g (2¾ oz) spanish onions
300g (1⅓ cups, 10 oz) pineapple pieces
300g (1⅓ cups, 10 oz) carrots
oil for frying

200ml (6½ fl oz) pineapple juice
5ml (1 teaspoon) white vinegar
20g (1 tablespoon, ½ oz) tomato puree
5g sugar
2g ginger, ground
dash Worcestershire sauce
10g (2 teaspoons, ⅓ oz) cornflour
sesame seeds to garnish
steamed rice to serve

create

Cut the tofu into bite-sized cubes and season. Coat with flour, dip into beaten egg and deep-fry until just brown.

Cut onions and seeded capsicums into 3cm (1 inch) squares. Cut carrots on the diagonal (bite-sized).

Sauté the vegetables, making sure to retain their crispness. Remove from heat and set aside.

Drain the pineapple and reserve juice for sauce. Sauté pineapple lightly and set aside separately.

To make the sauce, heat pineapple juice, vinegar, tomato puree, sugar, ginger and Worcestershire sauce until well combined. Blend the cornflour and cold water to make a paste, then add to the sauce to thicken it to a light consistency. Stir constantly.

Combine the pineapple and vegetables in a pan and sauté quickly to heat through. Next add sufficient sauce to just glaze the pieces and serve on a bed of steamed rice with a sprinkling of sesame seeds on top.

Note: If using fresh pineapple, dice and bring to the boil in a little water and use in the same way as tinned pineapple. The tofu can be marinated in soy sauce for an hour to add extra flavour if you prefer.

feast

Savoury and sweet, sure to delight all palates.

gourmet vegetarian patties

Preparation Time: 30 minutes   Cooking Time: 40 minutes   Serves: 6

250g (1 cup, 8 oz) sweet
potato
250g (1 cup, 8 oz) pontiac
potato
250g (1 cup, 8 oz) pumpkin
250g (1 cup, 8 oz) swede
1 clove garlic
2 sprigs of rosemary
oil for roasting
2 eggs
50g (1cup, 2 oz) breadcrumbs,
dried
200g (6 oz) fresh mixed herbs,
chopped

Preheat oven to 200°C (400°F, Gas Mark 6).

Cut vegetables into rough cubes and roast with garlic and rosemary in a hot oven, 25–35 minutes. When cooked, drain well and cool, then puree all ingredients with the fresh herbs.

Combine with beaten eggs and breadcrumbs, add more breadcrumbs if mix is too wet.

Shape into patties and fry in butter and oil. Drain on absorbent paper.

Serve two patties on a mound of hummus, accompanied by a mix of rocket, spanish onions and cherry tomatoes.

hearty home-style lasagne

Preparation Time: 1 hour   Cooking Time: 1 hour   Serves: 4

gather

1kg (4 cups, 2.2 lb)
roasted vegetables
(e.g. potato, sweet
potato, turnip, swede)
1 bunch rosemary,
finely diced
12 tomatoes, roasted
500g (2 cups, 1.1 lb)
roasted tomato puree
1 bunch basil,
chopped
2 red capsicums
(sweet peppers),
peeled and roasted
1 onion, sliced
oil for roasting and
pan-frying
300g (1$\frac{1}{3}$ cups, 10 oz)
mozzarella cheese
cracked pepper
salt
12 sheets dried
lasagne

create

Preheat oven to 200°C (400°F, Gas Mark 6).

Peel and cut root vegetables into bite-sized chunks, brush with oil and sprinkle with rosemary, salt and pepper and roast for 30–45 minutes.

Brush tomatoes with oil and roast in oven until softened, about 30–45 minutes. Remove from heat and when cool, dice 4 of the tomatoes into rough cubes and set aside. Puree remaining tomatoes and set aside.

Cut roasted capsicums into squares. Pan-fry onion.

Cook pasta sheets in a large quantity of boiling water. Remove and refresh in cold water. Store in water until ready to assemble.

To assemble lasagne, place diced roasted tomatoes in oven-proof dish or on a tray. Lay a sheet of cooked pasta over the tomatoes then a layer of roasted vegetables. Add basil, red capsicum, onions and cover with tomato puree. Repeat for next layer then finish with a pasta sheet on top.

Reduce heat to 180°C (350°F, Gas Mark 4), smother lasagne with mozzarella cheese, sprinkle with black pepper and bake for about 30 minutes until well heated and cheese is golden in colour.

feast

Easy to prepare ahead then cook and serve when company drops in. Serve with salad and fresh crusty garlic bread. It is also good to freeze.

wild rice & brown rice nut salad with citrus sauce

Preparation Time: 10 minutes   Cooking Time: 60 minutes   Serves: 6   **Vegan**

gather

Salad

250g (1 cup, 8 oz) wild rice

250g (1 cup, 8 oz) brown rice

500g (2 cups, 16 oz) chopped pecan nuts (or your choice of nut)

20ml (1 tablespoon, ½ fl oz) oil or nut butter

2 small onions, finely chopped

2 sticks celery, finely chopped

2 cloves garlic, crushed

½ bunch lemon thyme

2 sprigs basil

12 green shallots, chopped

2 teaspoons fresh ginger, grated

3 oranges, peeled and cut into segments

Sauce

500ml (2 cups, 17 fl oz) orange juice

80ml ($^1/_3$ cup, 2½ fl oz) lemon juice

80ml ($^1/_3$ cup, 2½ fl oz) lime juice

125ml (½ cup, 4 fl oz) cold water

2 teaspoons arrowroot (blended with water)

salt and pepper

create

Cook wild rice in a large pan of rapidly boiling water for 45–60 minutes or until rice looks ready to explode.

Cook brown rice separately in a large pan of rapidly boiling water.

When rice is tender, drain and rinse through with cold water.

Toast pecans on oven tray in a moderate oven for about 5 minutes.

Heat butter/oil in a pan, add onion, celery and garlic, sauté until onion is soft. Place in large bowl, mix in both rices, shallots, ginger, orange segments and toasted pecans.

To make the sauce, combine ingredients in a saucepan and boil to reduce until it is the required consistency. Extra juice can be added if it becomes too thick.

feast

A great salad on its own, served in lettuce cups or as an accompaniment to Tofu Skewers (see page 57).

corn & potato chowder

Preparation Time: 10 minutes   Cooking Time: 45–60 minutes   Serves: 10   **Gluten-free Vegan**

gather

3 cobs corn

2 onions

2 gloves garlic

4–5 potatoes cut into small
equal sized cubes

4-5 sweet potatoes
(kumara) cut into small
equal sized cubes

1 carrot, diced into small
equal-sized cubes (as above)

1 bay leaf

1 teaspoon fresh rosemary
or ½ teaspoon dried
rosemary

1 bunch fresh basil or
2 teaspoons dry basil

500ml (2 cups, 17f l oz)
vegetable stock with a little
sugar

500ml (2 cups, 17 fl oz)
cream (not included in
vegan version*)

salt and pepper

oil for frying

*for vegan option, replace
cream with extra stock or
soy milk

create

Remove corn kernels from cobs and set aside. Retain corn cobs for flavour during the cooking process.

Sauté onions, potatoes, carrots and garlic for 5 minutes. Add fresh rosemary, corn kernels and bay leaf. Cook for another 5 minutes. Add chopped basil and homemade stock (or a good quality store-bought stock equivalent). Add corn cobs but remove before adding cream.

Bring to a boil then simmer for 30 minutes. When potatoes break down, remove corn cobs and add cream if using. Add salt and pepper to taste.

feast

A hearty dish that everyone will enjoy, served with fresh bread.

nut & bean croquettes

Preparation Time: 24 hours   Cooking Time: 30 minutes   Serves: 10   **Vegan**

gather

Croquettes

500g (2 cups, 1 lb) chickpeas
(soak in water for 24 hours,
changing water twice)
500g (2 cups, 1 lb) soy beans
(soak in water for 24 hours,
changing water twice)
500g (2 cups, 1 lb) potatoes
1 bunch English spinach, chopped
2 spanish onions, diced
3 cloves garlic, diced
125g (½ cup, 4 oz) tahini paste
60g (¼ cup, 2 oz) sweet chilli
1 bunch coriander (cilantro),
chopped
salt and pepper to taste
500–750g (2–3 cups, 16–24 oz)
crushed nuts (equal measures
walnuts, hazelnuts and peanuts)
flour for rolling croquettes
vegetable oil for deep frying

Sauce

2kg (4 lb) roma tomatoes
250ml (1 cup, 8 fl oz) olive oil
100ml (3½ fl oz) balsamic vinegar
salt and pepper
bunch fresh oregano

create

Preheat oven to 200°C (400°F, Gas Mark 6).

Boil chickpeas and soy beans until tender. Drain.
Boil potatoes until tender and drain.

Finely chop onions and garlic, sauté in oil and
drain.

Blend potatoes, peas and beans with garlic, onion,
coriander, chilli and tahini paste until smooth.

Fold spinach into mix. Season to taste.

The mixture should be firm enough to allow you
to shape it into the required size. Roll croquettes
in flour and coat with crushed nuts then deep-fry.

Sauce

Cut tomatoes into quarters and coat with olive
oil and balsamic vinegar. Sprinkle with salt and
pepper. Place on tray and roast in oven for
30 minutes or until golden brown.

Blend tomatoes when cool with fresh oregano.
Season with salt and pepper, adjust consistency
with a little water. Reheat before serving.

feast

The croquettes can be served hot or cold.

eggplant roulade

Preparation Time: 30 minutes   Cooking Time: 15 minutes   Serves: 6

(see page 45)

gather

Roulade

1 large eggplant (aubergine)
250g (1 cup, 8 oz) blue vein cheese
2 spring onions
220g (7 oz) breadcrumbs
1 bunch sage
2 tablespoons olive tapenade
10 sun-dried tomatoes, thinly sliced
salt and pepper
2 red capsicums (sweet peppers), roasted and peeled
1 clove garlic

create

Char-grill (broil) thinly sliced eggplant.

Fry spring onions, sage, garlic and pepper.

Remove from heat. Add breadcrumbs to reduce moisture and thicken mixture.

Lay out eggplant, spread with a layer of cheese and tapenade and then cover with a layer of breadcrumb mix. Finally sprinkle sliced sun-dried tomatoes over mix.

Roll to form a log, wrap with plastic film and allow to stand for 15 minutes.

Sauce

To create the sauce, puree roasted red capsicums (see page 45), adjust consistency with a little water and season to taste.

Cut roulade and drizzle with sauce to serve.

feast

Enjoy the rich taste of blue vein cheese. Great served with crusty bread.

warm asparagus, orange & potato salad

Preparation Time: 15 minutes   Cooking Time: 15 minutes   Serves: 4   **Gluten-free Vegan**

gather

150ml (5 fl oz) orange juice
200ml (6½ fl oz) olive oil
24 asparagus spears
2 oranges segmented
1 bunch (2 tablespoons)
fresh lemon thyme leaves
12 chat (small) potatoes,
boiled and cooled
freshly ground black pepper
and sea salt

Turkish bread to serve
(not included for
gluten-free option)

create

To make the sauce, heat orange juice, lemon thyme, salt and pepper then cool slightly and add olive oil. Whisk until combined.

Cut 1–2cm (about an inch) off base of asparagus spears and place them into boiling water. Cook for 3–5 minutes until tender.

Remove the asparagus spears from the water and drain.

Blanch cooked potatoes to warm, then drain.

feast

Place asparagus spears, orange segments and chat potatoes on pre-warmed plates and cover with the dressing. Serve with toasted turkish bread.

pear, parmesan & walnut salad

Preparation Time: 10 minutes   Cooking Time: 4 minutes   Serves: 4   **Gluten-free**

gather

2 ripe pears, cored and sliced
200g (6½ oz) baby lettuce leaves and mesclun mix
100g (½ cup, 3½ oz) walnuts, roasted
50g (1¾ oz) parmesan cheese, shaved with vegetable peeler

100ml (3½ fl oz) balsamic vinegar
200ml (7 fl oz) olive oil
30ml (6 teaspoons, 1 fl oz) lime juice
salt and pepper

create

Preheat oven to 200°C (400°F, Gas Mark 6).

Roast walnuts in oven for 4 minutes.

Make vinaigrette by combining vinegar, oil, lime juice, salt and pepper. Shake well before using.

Combine salad leaves and vinaigrette in place in a bowl. Toss.

Arrange sliced pears on salad leaves, top with roasted walnuts and shaved parmesan.

feast

Vary the quantities of the ingredients according to your preference.

warm tomato tart with three cheeses

Preparation Time: 45 minutes   Cooking Time: 30 minutes   Serves: 4

gather

Pastry

185g (6¼ oz) plain flour
100g (½ cup, 3½ oz)
butter, chilled and diced
1 egg yolk
30ml (6 teaspoons,
1 fl oz) iced water
10–15 basil leaves to
line pastry

Filling

6–8 roma tomatoes,
skins removed, cut
lengthwise and seeded
sea salt and black
pepper, freshly ground
2 tablespoons fresh
oregano leaves,
chopped
180g (¾ cup, 6 oz)
parmesan cheese,
freshly grated
200g (7 oz) mascarpone
2 egg yolks
2 tablespoons fresh basil
leaves
100g (½ cup, 3½ oz)
gruyere, grated

create

Preheat oven to 180°C (350°F, Gas Mark 4).

For the pastry, sift flour into a bowl with a pinch of salt. Use a mixer with a dough hook or rub in butter with fingertips until mixture resembles breadcrumbs. Make a well in the centre, mix in egg yolk then add water slowly until dough is pliable. Wrap and chill for 30 minutes.

Roll out the pastry and line 4 greased and floured 10cm tins. Prick pastry evenly with a fork. Line tarts with baking paper and bake blind (see page 37) for 12 minutes. Remove from heat and allow to cool.

For the filling, cut tomatoes in half lengthwise and brush halves with oil and place on an oven tray. Lightly season with sea salt and freshly ground black pepper, sprinkle with oregano and basil and lightly cover with some of the parmesan. Grill until light brown. Set aside and allow to cool.

In a bowl, mix mascarpone with 2 egg yolks, then fold in grated gruyere and a little salt and pepper.

To assemble, line tart shell with basil leaves. Place cheese mix on top. Cover again with basil leaves then place cooked tomatoes on top to cover. Sprinkle lightly with remaining parmesan and bake tarts for 10–15 minutes.

feast

Garnish with herb sprigs and serve warm with a rocket (arugula) salad.

lemon, lentil & coriander soup

Preparation Time: 20 minutes   Cooking Time: 10 minutes   Serves: 6   **Gluten-free Vegan**

gather

400g (13 oz) red lentils
1 L (4 cups, 34 fl oz)
vegetable stock
zest of 3 lemons
3 bunches coriander
(cilantro)
4 spring onions,
chopped
½ teaspoon five spice
salt and pepper

create

Wash and rinse lentils. Combine all ingredients in a pot and bring to the boil. Reduce heat to a simmer and allow lentils to soften.

Blend in a food processor. Season with salt and pepper to taste.

feast

A great soup as is or you can add cream before serving (and/or chilli for extra heat). This soup will also freeze well.

potato timbale with roasted cashews & lemon garlic cream sauce

Preparation Time: 40 minutes   Cooking Time: 60 minutes   Serves: 4–6   **Gluten-free**

gather

Timbale

1kg (4 cups, 2.2 lb) pontiac
potatoes, peeled and cut in
equal sizes
40g (1 oz) butter, melted
2 tablespoons curry powder
125ml (½ cup, 4 fl oz) sour
cream
2–3 eggs
1 teaspoon cumin/garam
masala
1 teaspoon turmeric
salt and pepper

Sauce

250–500ml (1–2 cups,
8–16 fl oz) cream
30ml (6 teaspoons, 1 fl oz)
lemon juice
1 clove garlic, finely
chopped
100g (½ cup, 3½ oz)
cashews

create

Preheat oven to 180°C (350°F, Gas Mark 4).

Boil potatoes until just tender then drain and allow to dry. Sieve or process potatoes until smooth but not sloppy. Do not overblend.

In a saucepan melt the butter on a low heat and add garlic, curry, turmeric, cumin/garam marsala and cook for 2–3 minutes. Remove from heat and allow to cool. Add into potato mix.

Beat eggs and sour cream together and fold into potato mix.

Oil individual timbale or cup-shaped moulds then fill with potato mix. Place moulds in a baking dish and bake in a bain-marie for up to 1 hour or until cooked. Set aside.

For the sauce, roast cashews in oven for 2–3 minutes at 200°C (400°F). In a pan, fry chopped garlic, add cream, salt and pepper and reduce over medium heat until thick and glossy. Stir in lemon juice.

feast

To serve, invert mould on a plate and ladle with cream sauce. Garnish with roasted cashews.

for the passionate

Good times, good friends and good food—I can't think of a better way to fulfil a passion that I believe we all share—scrumptious, fulfilling meals and the time to enjoy it with those we love.

For the passionate who journey through this chapter, I hope you enjoy the experience of creating a truly fabulous dish—a reward to the senses every step of the way.

Compliments await you, so why not gather your loved ones and a bottle of wine, turn the music up loud and cook for your crowd.

roasted pumpkin & rocket gnocchi

Preparation Time: 30–45 minutes   Cooking Time: 1 hour+   Serves: 4–6   **Vegan**

gather

Caramelised Onions

30ml (6 teaspoons, 1 fl oz) oil

3 brown onions, sliced

150g (5 oz) brown sugar

30ml (6 teaspoons, 1 fl oz) vinegar

Gnocchi

1 small butternut pumpkin, peeled, cut and roasted

6 desiree or pontiac potatoes, peeled and cut into equal sizes

500g (2 cups, 1.1 lb) flour

salt and pepper

Sauce

12 tomatoes for roasting, skins removed

30g (6 teaspoons, 1 oz) sage, chopped

2 bunches rocket (arugula), chopped

1 clove garlic, chopped

salt and pepper

200g (7 oz) parmesan cheese (not included in vegan option)

olive oil for roasting and preparation

Preheat oven to 200°C (400°F, Gas Mark 6).

Heat oil in a large pan and add sliced onions, covering the entire surface. Sprinkle all the sugar over the onions to cover completely. Do not stir or move the onions. Allow to cook on low–medium heat for 30–45 minutes or until golden. Stir in vinegar and cook for 2–3 minutes more. Set aside.

Peel and cut butternut pumpkin into even pieces and place on baking tray. Coat pieces in a light cover of olive oil, salt and pepper. Roast for 30–45 minutes. Remove and cool.

Roast tomatoes in oven for 30–45 minutes until well coloured. Set aside for gnocchi sauce.

Peel and cut potatoes into even pieces and drop into boiling water. Cook until tender, remove and drain. Allow to dry then run the pieces through a ricer (to mash) or blend in food processor.

Add cooked, cooled pumpkin and blend or mash as above.

Gently pan-fry rocket with salt, pepper and crushed garlic. Set aside.

Transfer potato and pumpkin into a bowl, mix through a quarter of the rocket mix (retain remainder for serving), then fold in flour, one-quarter at a time.

Coat hands in oil and roll all the gnocchi mix into balls. Place on tray. Roll the gnocchi balls in flour and roll in hands again for at least 30 seconds each to work in the gluten. Set aside on tray.

The sauce is created by blending the roasted tomatoes and sage. Heat through in frypan.

Drop the gnocchi into boiling water until they rise to the top. Remove from water and place in tomato sauce. Sprinkle parmesan on top and bake until golden (for 20-30 minutes).

Serve with rocket salad and caramelised onions.

goat's cheese roulade

Preparation Time: 15–20 minutes   Cooking Time: 15 minutes   Serves: 4–6   **Gluten-free**

4 red capsicums (sweet peppers), roasted and peeled
200g (7 oz) goat's cheese, room temperature, crumbled
1 bunch basil leaves
oil

Preheat grill (broiler).

Top and tail capsicums, de-seed but keep whole. Brush skin with oil and blacken under grill until blistered. Seal in a plastic bag and leave for 5 minutes. Peel the capsicums, keeping them whole.

Lay capsicums lengthwise on a clean tea towel, creating a rectangle, 25cm x 35cm long.

Meanwhile, pick the leaves off the basil and lay on top of the capsicum layer, overlapping the leaves slightly, shiny side down.

Using damp hands, crumble goat's cheese lightly over basil, covering all the area.

Using the tea towel as a guide, gently roll capsicums into a cylinder, then wrap in plastic film and tightly twist ends. Chill on a tray in refrigerator.

Cut into rounds to serve.

savoury mushroom pancakes

Preparation Time: 30 minutes   Cooking Time: 10 minutes   Serves: 6–8

Pancakes

250g (1 cup, 8 oz) plain flour
125g (½ cup, 4 oz) coarse polenta
½ teaspoon baking powder
½ teaspoon bicarbonate of soda
2 cloves garlic, finely diced
10 basil leaves, finely shredded
250ml (1 cup, 8 fl oz) milk
1 egg
500g (2 cups, 1.1 lb) mushrooms,* diced
60g (¼ cup, 2 oz) parmesan cheese
salt and pepper
butter for frying

Filling

500g (2 cups, 1.1 lb) mushrooms,* diced
1 bunch english spinach (stems removed)
100g (½ cup, 3½ oz) fresh herbs of your choice
sesame oil for stir-frying

Sauce

2 spring onions
2 bunches english spinach (stems removed)
8 basil leaves
250ml (1 cup, 8 fl oz) vegetable stock (homemade if possible)
salt and pepper
* Almost any combination of mushrooms can be used, we suggest button, oyster, shimeji and enoki.

Combine flour, polenta, baking powder and bicarbonate of soda. Add garlic and basil. Mix in milk, then whisk in egg, then add mushrooms and parmesan cheese. Add salt and pepper to taste. Rest for 10 minutes (the mixture, not yourself) before cooking pancakes in a frying pan with a little butter until golden brown.

Simply stir-fry your preferred variety of mushrooms with sesame oil, fresh herbs and one-third of the spinach to make the filling.

For the sauce, dice onions and fry with a little butter until soft, add basil leaves and the rest of the spinach. Fry for 1 minute or until wilted. (Hold aside a little of the wilted spinach leaves for garnish.) Add stock slowly and blend thoroughly. Add salt and pepper to taste. Cool and puree. Add the retained wilted spinach leaves if wanted or add as final garnish.

To serve, place pancake on a plate, rest mushroom filling on top, then top with second pancake and pour the spinach sauce over it.

mediterranean eggplant & goat's cheese tower

Preparation Time: 45 minutes   Cooking Time: 1 hour   Serves: 4–6   **Gluten-free**

gather

2 large aubergines (eggplants), cut into 1–2cm (about 1 inch) rounds

2 red capsicums (sweet peppers), roasted and skins removed

1 sweet potato, peeled and cut into 1cm rounds

1 bunch english spinach

12 basil leaves

250g (1 cup, 8 oz) roasted tomatoes

250g (1 cup, 8 oz) fresh goat's cheese, crumbled

3 tablespoons ground cumin

olive oil

plum sauce (available in good food stores)

create

Preheat oven to 190°C (375°F, Gas Mark 5).

Spike eggplants with a fork all over and on both sides. Brush both sides with olive oil and sprinkle cumin over oiled surfaces. Place on a baking tray and bake. Turn eggplants over when brown (about 10–15 minutes), allow other side to brown then remove and allow to cool.

Reduce oven heat to 180°C (350°F, Gas Mark 4). Peel and slice sweet potato into thin rounds and roast in oven for 30–45 minutes till brown.

Roast and peel capsicum halves and remove skins.

Wash and discard stems of spinach. Blanch in boiling water for 5 seconds. Remove, drain and cool.

To assemble each tower, layer ingredients on a baking tray starting with roasted tomato, then a slice of cooked eggplant, top with fresh basil leaves, then goat's cheese. Continue with layers of roasted tomato, eggplant, sweet potato and goat's cheese. Next layer spinach, roasted capsicum and finish with eggplant.

Place baking tray in oven until towers are heated through.

feast

Serve with a good plum sauce drizzled over the towers.

three cheese cannelloni

Preparation Time: 20–30 minutes   Cooking Time: 20–30 minutes   Serves: 6

gather

12 cannelloni shells (fresh),
2 per person

Filling

2 eggs
½ bunch fresh mint, finely chopped
½ bunch fresh oregano,
finely chopped
½ bunch fresh lemon thyme,
finely chopped
½ bunch fresh rosemary,
finely chopped
250g (1 cup, 8 oz) parmesan cheese,
grated
250g (1 cup, 8 oz) gruyere cheese,
crumbled
250g (1 cup, 8 oz) mascarpone
salt and freshly ground pepper

Sauce

60ml (¼ cup, 2 fl oz) balsamic
vinegar
185ml (¾ cup, 6 fl oz) olive oil
10–12 tomatoes

250g (1 cup, 8 oz) parmesan cheese,
grated

create

Preheat oven to 180°C (350°F, Gas Mark 4).

Combine eggs, mint, oregano, thyme, rosemary, ¾ teaspoon salt, pepper and three cheeses. Mix well. Roll into logs and place in refrigerator to stand.

Blanch the fresh pasta shells in boiling salted water for 30 seconds. Immediately remove and place in bowl of iced water with 2 tablespoons olive oil. Drain on slightly damp clean kitchen towels, cover well.

To make the sauce, first make a marinade from 1 part balsamic vinegar to 3 parts olive/vegetable oil and mix well. Cut tomatoes in half and brush with marinade. Roast on baking tray in a hot oven for 30 minutes or until golden roasted. Puree with marinade in a food processor and the sauce is ready to use.

Fill cannelloni tubes with cheese filling. Place in oiled ovenproof dish, cover with roasted tomato sauce and top with parmesan. Bake until hot and bubbling around edges, approximately 20 minutes.

feast

If using store-bought pasta, baking times will vary. Follow instructions on the pack.

warm beetroot & orange salad with nasturtium leaves

Preparation Time: 20–30 minutes   Cooking Time: 20–30 minutes   Serves: 6   **Gluten-free Vegan**

gather

12 baby beetroot and leaves

15 nasturtium leaves

200g (7 oz) baby spinach leaves

80ml ($^{1}/_{3}$ cup, 2½ fl oz) balsamic vinegar

80ml ($^{1}/_{3}$ cup, 2½ fl oz) orange juice

2 oranges, zest and segments

160ml ($^{2}/_{3}$ cup, 5½ fl oz) olive oil

100g (½ cup, 3½ oz) roasted walnut halves

100g (½ cup, 3½ oz) cashews

2 tablespoons chives, finely chopped

salt and pepper

create

Preheat oven to 100°C (250°F, Gas Mark 1).

Cut leaves from beets and wash in cold water, then drain. Wash beets and place in boiling water until tender (when a skewer can be inserted with ease). Drain, cool slightly, then peel. Cut beetroot into small wedges and place in a baking dish.

Combine balsamic vinegar, orange juice, orange zest, olive oil, salt and pepper. Whisk together and pour half over beetroots.

Cover baking tray with foil and bake beetroot wedges in oven for 30 minutes or until tender.

Toss remaining ingredients—beetroot, nasturtium and spinach leaves, orange segments, walnuts, cashews and chives—with the remaining dressing.

feast

Arrange mix on a plate or platter and place beetroots randomly in salad. Cocktail potatoes could also be used—boiled, drained and pan-fried until golden and added with oregano to the salad.

parmesan tart with fetta & caramelised onions

Preparation Time: 40 minutes   Cooking Time: 40 minutes   Serves: 4

gather

Pastry

375g (1 ½ cups, 12 oz)
plain flour
125g (½ cup, 4 oz)
parmesan cheese, grated
100g (½ cup, 3½ oz)
unsalted butter, chopped
1 egg yolk
40ml (2 tablespoons,
1³/₅ fl oz) iced water

Filling

10–15 onions, sliced
375g (1 ½ cups, 12 oz)
brown sugar
butter and oil
180g (¾ cup, 6 oz) fetta
cheese, crumbled

create

Preheat oven to 180°C (350°F, Gas Mark 4).

The pastry tart is made by combining flour and parmesan cheese in a blender (for a short time only) or by hand. Add butter to blender and pulse until combined and resembles breadcrumbs. Add egg yolk and pulse again. Add ice-cold water to bind, a few drops at a time. Do not over-pulse.

Wrap and refrigerate for 30 minutes.

Grease and flour tart tins. Roll out the pastry and line the tins. Prick pastry evenly with a fork. Line with baking paper, weight with baking beans and bake blind for 30 minutes (see page 37) or until golden.

To caramelise the onions, heat oil and butter in a pan. Add sliced onions but do not stir. Cover with brown sugar and allow to caramelise for 15–20 minutes. Remove from heat.

Spoon cooled onions into tart cases, top with crumbled fetta and return to oven or grill to colour and heat through.

feast

Great on their own or served with a fresh garden salad.

carrot crepes with rosemary & tomato jam

Preparation Time: 30 minutes   Cooking Time: 15 minutes   Serves: 4–6

gather

500g (2 cups, 16 oz)
plain flour
350ml (1½ cups, 12 fl oz)
milk
2 eggs
2 tablespoons butter
1 teaspoon garlic
salt and pepper
3 baby carrots, peeled and
grated (squeeze out as
much juice as you can)

butter and oil for frying

create

Place all ingredients except the carrots in a food processor and blend until smooth.

Place in a bowl and allow to stand for 30 minutes. Fold in squeezed carrots.

In a crepe pan or shallow frypan, heat 1 teaspoon of butter and 1 teaspoon of oil.

Pour a ladle of the crepe mix into the pan and tilt pan to allow mix to thinly cover base.

Cook for 1–2 minutes and flip crepe. Cook for a further minute and remove. Place on greaseproof paper while cooking remaining crepes.

Repeat until all the mixture is cooked.

feast

Serve with Tomato & Rosemary Jam
(see page 20).

stuffed zucchinis with english spinach sauce

Preparation Time: 30–40 minutes   Cooking Time: 30 minutes   Serves: 4

gather

8 yellow or green
 zucchinis (courgettes)
2 per person depending
on size
6 spanish onions
500g (2 cups, 1.1 lb)
tomato puree
1kg (4 cups, 2.2 lb) button
mushrooms, finely diced
3 cloves garlic
250g (1 cup, 8 oz) mixed
herbs (rosemary, sage, mint,
thyme, basil)
250g (1 cup, 8 oz) parmesan
cheese
oil for frying
salt and pepper

Sauce
2 spring onions
3 bunches english spinach
(stems removed)
8 basil leaves
250ml (1 cup, 8 fl oz)
vegetable stock
(homemade if possible)
salt and pepper

create

Preheat oven to 180°C (350°F, Gas Mark 4)

Sauté diced mushrooms, remove and drain.

Cut zucchinis in half and hull out gently, retain hulls and
flesh.

Fry onion and zucchini flesh until brown, add garlic and
herbs and stir well. Add tomato puree and bring to a
gentle simmer. Remove from heat and fold in sautéed
mushrooms. Season with salt and pepper.

Blanch hulled out zucchinis then fill with prepared mix
sprinkle with grated parmesan cheese and bake in oven
for 20-30 minutes.

For the sauce, dice onions and fry with a little butter
until soft, add basil leaves and all of the spinach. Fry for
1 minute or until wilted. (Hold aside a little of the wilted
spinach leaves for garnish.) Add stock slowly and blend
thoroughly. Add salt and pepper to taste. Cool and puree.
Add the retained wilted spinach leaves if you want to, or
add as final garnish.

feast

A tasty dish served on a bed of english spinach sauce.

chickpea & roasted root vegetable gratin

Preparation Time: 24 hours   Cooking Time: 40–45 minutes   Serves: 4   **Gluten-free Vegan**

gather

2 sweet potatoes, chopped
into cubes
250g (1 cup, 8 oz) dry
chickpeas, covered with water
and soaked overnight
750g (3 cups, 1.5 lb) eggplant,
not peeled
40ml (2 tablespoons,
1³/₅ fl oz) olive oil
1 medium onion, minced
2 garlic cloves, minced
2 tablespoons fresh parsley,
chopped
½ teaspoon fresh thyme,
chopped
1 red capsicum, cut, seeded
and roasted
1.5kg (6 cups, 3.3 lb)
tomatoes, roasted
½ teaspoon ground cumin
12–15 fresh basil leaves, torn
into pieces
salt and freshly ground black
pepper
vegetable oil for deep-frying
and shallow-frying
500g (2 cups, 1.1 lb) parmesan
cheese, grated (not included in
vegan option)

create

Preheat oven to 180°C (350°F, Gas Mark 4).

Pick over the chickpeas and discard any stones. Cover with water and soak overnight. Next day, drain and place in a saucepan with enough water to cover. Bring to the boil then reduce heat and simmer until light and fluffy. Drain and cool.

Brush capsicum and tomatoes with oil and roast in oven. Dice capsicum and cut tomatoes when cool.

Cut eggplant into 2.5cm (1 inch) cubes. Place cubes in a colander and salt lightly. Leave to drain for 30 minutes. Rinse and pat very dry with paper towels. Deep-fry, drain well and set aside.

Cut sweet potato into 2.5cm (1 inch) cubes and deep-fry. Drain and set aside.

Add 2 tablespoons olive oil to the pan and sauté minced onion until soft. Add the garlic, parsley and thyme and sauté for 2 minutes. Add roasted capsicum and roasted tomatoes.

Combine mix with eggplant, sweet potato, chickpeas and basil. Season with salt and pepper and add a little ground cumin.

Place mixture in a large shallow gratin dish (or 4 individual moulds) and sprinkle with parmesan cheese. Bake until hot and golden, 40–45 minutes.

feast

A great winter dish! It can also be frozen and reheated for an easy meal.

pakoras

Preparation Time: 15 minutes   Cooking Time: 10 minutes   Serves: 4–6   **Gluten-free Vegan**

gather

500g (2 cups, 1.1 lb) chickpea flour
1 tablespoon garam masala
2 teaspoons salt and pepper
1 tablespoon curry powder
1 tablespoon turmeric
250ml (1 cup, 8 fl oz) water
4 garlic cloves, crushed
4–6 sweet potatoes, peeled, boiled until just firm, then mashed
2–3 pontiac potatoes, peeled, boiled until just firm, then mashed
1kg (4 cups, 2.2 lb) raw vegetables (spanish onions, corn, carrots, red capsicum, green beans, carrots), finely diced
oil

create

Sift flour and place with garam masala, salt, turmeric, curry and garlic into a food processor. Add water and process until smooth. Allow batter to stand for 15 minutes.

Add the prepared vegetables and stir to coat them evenly.

Heat oil and add teaspoonfuls of vegetable mixture to the oil. Cook until golden on both sides. Drain well.

Note: Do not add diced vegetables to batter until ready to cook, otherwise batter will become too runny. If batter becomes too runny, add more flour to it.

feast

Fritters can be refried to give a crisper coating.

cauliflower castle

gather

Castle

3 pontiac potatoes, peeled and cut into round slices

1 bunch fresh tarragon, finely shredded

oil for roasting

½ cauliflower, cut into flowerets

12 ruby chard leaves

30m (6 teaspoons, 1 fl oz) peanut oil

½ teaspoon palm sugar

2 punnets cherry tomatoes

30ml (6 teaspoons, 1 fl oz) balsamic vinegar

Roux

100g (½ cup, 3½ oz) flour

100g (½ cup, 3½ oz) butter

1 bunch fresh tarragon, finely shredded

50ml (1/5 cup, 1¾ fl oz) milk

3 bay leaves

1 cinnamon quill

10 peppercorns

6 cloves

1 teaspoon nutmeg

1 onion

80g (7 tablespoons, 3 oz) gruyere cheese, grated

1 egg

create

Preheat oven to 200°C (400°F, Gas Mark 6).

Bake potatoes with oil, shredded tarragon, salt and pepper.

Blanch flowerets of cauliflower, drain well.

Wilt ruby chard in a hot frypan with peanut oil and palm sugar.

Coat cherry tomatoes in oil and sear until semi-soft then add balsamic vinegar and caramelise. Remove from heat and cool, then strain.

Melt butter with tarragon, add flour and cook to form a roux. Heat milk, onion, cinnamon, peppercorns, bay leaves, nutmeg and cloves—strain and add slowly to roux, stirring consistently to avoid lumps. Add grated gruyere, allow to thicken and remove from heat. Cool slightly, beat in the egg.

Grease and line base and sides of a tall cylindrical mould (or coffee mug) with baking paper. Place a layer of baked potatoes, then a thin layer of roux, 6–8 cherry tomatoes and then another layer of roux, then potatoes, then more roux. Top with cauliflower, then roux again, then ruby chard leaves, roux and potato layer to finish.

Place moulds in a baking tray and bake for 30 minutes.

Serve with Béarnaise Sauce (see page 24)

feast

To serve, invert mould on a plate and lift it off. Remove baking paper and ladle generously with Béarnaise Sauce. Serve immediately.

thai-style tofu salad with fresh soba noodles

Preparation Time: 30 minutes   Cooking Time: No cooking   Serves: 4   **Vegan**

gather

Salad

120ml (½ cup, 4 fl oz) vegetable oil

500g (2 cups, 1.1 lb) tofu, cubed

375g packet fresh soba noodles

3 bunches fresh asparagus

3 medium carrots, peeled and julienned

2 large red peppers, thinly sliced

Dressing

3 small fresh red chillies, seeded and chopped

250ml (1 cup, 8 fl oz) lime juice (8 limes)

130g (1/3 cup) brown sugar, firmly packed

2 tablespoons tamari (soy sauce)

2 stems fresh lemongrass, finely chopped

create

Heat oil in pan, add tofu and fry until golden and firm.

Add noodles to a pan of boiling water and boil uncovered for about 5 minutes or until tender. Rinse under cold water, drain well and cut into 15cm (6 inch) lengths.

Boil, steam or microwave asparagus until just tender (about 3–6 minutes depending on method used). Drain and rinse well under cold water.

Combine tofu, noodles, asparagus, carrots and peppers in a large bowl.

Combine dressing ingredients and mix well. Toss through salad.

feast

This recipe can be made three hours ahead. Store covered in the refrigerator. It is not suitable to freeze.

twice baked goat's cheese soufflé

Preparation Time: 30 minutes   Cooking Time: 55 minutes   Serves: 4

400ml (1¾ cups, 14 fl oz) milk

250g (1 cup, 8 oz) onions, sliced

2 cloves, crushed or chopped

pinch of nutmeg

2 bay leaves

150g (5 oz) butter

150g (5 oz) flour

500g (2 cups, 1.1 lb) goat's cheese, crumbled

6 egg yolks

8 egg whites

1 teaspoon salt

pepper

Preheat oven to 180°C (350°F, Gas Mark 4).

Combine milk, onions, bay leaves, cloves and nutmeg in a saucepan and bring to the boil, then strain and allow to cool

Melt butter in a saucepan add flour and make a blond roux. Whisk in milk. Heat until thick. Add cheese and whisk in yolks. Add salt and pepper then cool.

Whisk egg whites to firm peaks then fold into mixture.

Divide into lightly buttered moulds. Bake in a tray with water, but no cover. The soufflés are cooked when they have risen and browned slightly, approximately 30–40 minutes. Remove from heat and allow to cool.

When ready to serve, preheat oven to 180°C (350°F, Gas Mark 4), place soufflés in a baking tray and reheat for 15 minutes to bake a second time.

This method of twice baking removes the last-minute fear of soufflé failure just prior to serving. The first bake stage can be done the day before serving. Serve with Lemon Garlic Cream Sauce (see page 85) if you want.

pumpkin & eggplant curry

Preparation Time: 30 minutes   Cooking Time: 45 minutes   Serves: 6–8   **Gluten-free Vegan**

gather

oil

2 spanish onions, chopped

2 cloves garlic, crushed

1 stem lemongrass, chopped finely

1–2 medium red chillies, chopped

1 knob fresh ginger, grated

1 bunch fresh coriander (cilantro), chopped

2 eggplants (aubergines), sliced and unpeeled

30g (6 teaspoons, 1 oz) ground cumin

2kg (8 cups, 4.4 lb) butternut pumpkin

12–15 baby or cocktail potatoes

375g (1½ cups, 12 oz) cooked chickpeas or red kidney beans

250ml (1 cup, 8 fl oz) well-flavoured vegetable stock

350ml (1½ cups, 12 fl oz) coconut milk

create

Preheat oven to 200°C (400°F, Gas Mark 6).

Heat oil, add onion, lemongrass, garlic, chillies, ginger and coriander and cook through.

Slice eggplants lengthwise into 2cm (1 inch) slices, brush with oil and sprinkle with ground cumin. Bake in oven for 30–40 minutes, turning halfway through. Cook until golden brown. Remove from oven, cool and cut into even cubes.

Peel, cut and de-seed the pumpkin, cut into even 3cm cubes. Place on a baking tray, coat with oil and season with salt and pepper. Roast in oven for 30–45 minutes. Remove and drain on absorbent paper.

Boil potatoes (skin on) until tender and a skewer can be easily removed when tested. Drain and cool, leave whole.

Combine all ingredients in a heavy-based saucepan and bring to the boil, then simmer for 20 minutes. Serve with jasmine or basmati rice.

feast

A guaranteed crowd-pleaser.

dreamy desserts & tempting treats

Don't we all love those sensuous moments when we delight in some forbidden morsel of saucy chocolate pudding, mesmerising meringue or citrus zing?

These recipes are too delicious to bother feeling guilty about, so why not indulge yourself and your friends. Whether a memorable end to the evening meal or a delicious mouthful of sweetness to complement an afternoon tea or coffee, everybody will love these desserts and tempting treats.

mango & pineapple cake with coconut

Preparation Time: 10–15 minutes   Cooking Time: 75 minutes   Serves: 8

425g can mango slices in light syrup, drained
(2–3 fresh mangoes)
125g (½ cup, 4 oz) unsalted butter, softened
120g (½ cup, 3¾ oz) castor sugar
½ vanilla bean (scraped) or 1 teaspoon vanilla essence
2 egg whites
440g can crushed pineapple in syrup
500g (2 cups, 1.1 lb) plain flour
1 teaspoon baking powder
250g (1 cup, 8 oz) desiccated coconut
sifted icing sugar to serve

Preheat oven to 160°C (325°F, Gas Mark 3).

Grease a 10 x 21cm (4 x 8 inch) loaf pan (base measurement) and line with baking paper.

Lightly puree mango slices in a food processor.

Beat butter, sugar and vanilla until light and fluffy in a medium bowl with electric beaters.

Combine flour and baking powder. Sift half of the flour into the mix, then add 1 egg white and beat well. Add remaining flour and remaining egg white, beating well.

Fold in mango, coconut and crushed pineapple.

Pour mixture into prepared cake pan and bake in preheated oven for 1¼ hours or until cooked. Allow cake to cool then turn out.

This can be made up to three days ahead. Store in an airtight container. Dust with icing sugar on the day of serving.

chocolate & hazelnut torte

Preparation Time: 15 minutes   Cooking Time: 30–60 minutes   Serves: 4   **Gluten-free**

gather

4 egg whites
275g (9 oz) castor sugar
½ teaspoon white vinegar
½ vanilla bean
25g hazelnuts, finely
chopped

2 punnets strawberries,
hulled and quartered
400g (13 oz) dark chocolate
125ml (½ cup, 4 fl oz) milk

250ml (1 cup, 8 fl oz)
thickened cream

create

Preheat oven to 100–120°C (250°F, Gas Mark 1).

Beat egg whites with whisk attachment on mixer until stiff peaks form. Slowly add sugar about 50g at a time. Allow mixture to incorporate the sugar till smooth (no granules) before adding next quantity of sugar. Continue whisking until all the sugar is incorporated and mixture is smooth, then add vanilla bean and vinegar. Whisk for 10 seconds.

Spoon 8 equal discs of mixture onto greaseproof paper and sprinkle with finely chopped hazelnuts. Bake for 30–60 minutes. Set aside when cooked.

Cut base and quarter strawberries. Set aside.

Whip thickened cream until soft peaks form. Set aside.

Melt chocolate and milk together in microwave in 5–10 second bursts, stirring after each burst. Allow to cool and set aside.

To assemble, place one baked meringue on a plate as a base. Spoon a generous amount of whipped cream on base then decorate with fresh strawberries. Top with more cream to secure and pour chocolate sauce over it. Top with second meringue and chocolate.

feast

A marvellous indulgence and well worth the effort.

your favourite ice-cream

Preparation Time: Day in advance   Cooking Time: 15–20 minutes   Serves: Makes 1 L (4 cups, 32 fl oz)   **Gluten-free**

gather

8 egg yolks
1 L (4 cups, 34 fl oz) cream
250g (1 cup, 8 oz) castor
sugar
1 vanilla bean
125ml (½ cup, 4 fl oz) milk

create

To create a basic but delicious vanilla ice-cream, whisk egg yolks over a double boiler and slowly add sugar. Continue whisking in small quantities of sugar, making sure each has dissolved before adding the next lot.

Heat cream, milk and vanilla bean—do not allow to boil.

Add cream to egg mix, then mix over low heat for 2 minutes. Strain and cool before churning for 40–60 minutes or until set.

Harvest Hint

You need an ice-cream machine for this recipe, available at good retailers in a domestic size and price.

feast

Variations: For a luscious chocolate ice-cream, add 100g melted dark chocolate. It must be added to mix at the same temperature. Almost any variation can be added to the basic vanilla recipe—roasted coconut, slivered almonds or coffee make delicious alternatives.

apple, raspberry & blueberry sorbet

Preparation Time: 40–60 minutes   Cooking Time: No cooking   Serves: Makes 1 L (4 cups, 32 fl oz)   **Gluten-free**   **Vegan**

gather

Apple & Cinnamon
1 L (4 cups, 34 fl oz)
apple juice
375g (1½ cups, 12 oz)
castor sugar
2 cinnamon quills (removed
before churning)

Raspberry
1kg (2.2 lb) raspberries
500g (2 cups, 1.1 lb)
castor sugar
1 L (4 cups, 34 fl oz) water

Blueberry
1kg (2.2 lb) blueberries
500g (2 cups, 1.1 lb)
castor sugar
1 L (4 cups, 34 fl oz) water

create

The base mix is very simple—place the sugar and liquid into a saucepan with your choice of flavouring. Bring to the boil and allow to cool before churning in an ice-cream making machine for 40–60 minutes or until set.

feast

Serve a scoop of each on a plate, garnished with mint leaves. Almost any fruit or berry can be used for this recipe—you are limited only by your imagination.

chocolate self-saucing pudding

Preparation Time: 20 minutes   Cooking Time: 45–60 minutes   Serves: 6

gather

Pudding

500g (2 cups, 1.1 lb) plain flour
2 teaspoons baking powder
60g (¼ cup, 2 oz) castor sugar
30g (¼ cup, 2 oz) swiss cocoa
30g (¼ cup, 2 oz) malted milk powder
250ml (1 cup, 8 fl oz) milk
60g (¼ cup, 2 oz) butter, melted
2 eggs, lightly beaten

Sauce

100g (½ cup, 3½ oz) dark chocolate, roughly chopped
500ml (2 cups, 17 fl oz) milk
30g (6 teaspoons, 1 oz) butter
250g (1 cup, 8 oz) brown sugar
30g (¼ cup, 2 oz) swiss cocoa, sifted
2 tablespoons cornflour or arrowroot
Swiss cocoa or icing sugar for dusting

create

Preheat oven to 180°C (350°F, Gas Mark 4).

For the batter, sift flour, baking powder, castor sugar, cocoa, and malted milk powder into a bowl. Melt butter and add to mix, then milk and beat until smooth. Next beat in eggs. Set aside.

To make the sauce, combine chocolate, milk and butter in a saucepan and heat gently until chocolate and butter form a smooth liquid. Combine brown sugar, cocoa and cornflour in a bowl, add chocolate mixture and stir well.

Pour sauce into individual greased moulds. Gently pour batter over sauce to form the pudding layer.

Place the moulds into a baking tray and bake for 45–60 minutes or until firm. Turn out on a plate and the sauce will run over the sponge.

feast

Dust the cooked pudding with swiss cocoa or icing sugar.

citron tart

gather

165g (5½ oz) plain flour
125g (½ cup, 4 oz) icing sugar
100g (½ cup, 3½ oz) chilled butter, chopped
1 egg separated into yolk and white

6 eggs
250g (1 cup, 8 oz) castor sugar
2½ lemons, grated rind and strained juice
200ml (7 fl oz) pouring cream
icing sugar to serve

create

Preheat oven to 200°C (400°F, Gas Mark 6).

For pastry, combine flour and icing sugar in a food processor and process for 5 seconds.

Add butter and rub in with your fingertips until it resembles breadcrumbs. Add egg yolk and mix with a fork, then add a little water until it pulls together as a firm ball. Turn pastry out on a lightly floured surface and flatten. Wrap in plastic, then rest in refrigerator for 30 minutes.

Roll out pastry thinly on a lightly floured surface. Grease and line a 23cm (9 inch) flan tin with removable base (or individual moulds), pressing pastry gently into the corners. Cover with plastic and rest again in refrigerator for an hour.

Line pastry with greaseproof paper and bake blind (see page 37) for 10–15 minutes. Remove paper and beans, brush with lightly beaten egg white and return to oven at 180°C (350°F, Gas Mark 4). Bake until light golden brown, remove and cool.

For the filling, combine eggs and sugar in a bowl and machine whisk for 4 minutes. Add grated lemon rind and juice and whisk for 3 minutes, and finally whisk in cream for 1 minute. Pour mixture into pastry case and bake at 160°C (325°F, Gas Mark 3) for 45 minutes until filling is just set.

feast

Serve at room temperature, sprinkled with icing sugar.

hot chocolate praline soufflé

Preparation Time: 30 minutes   Cooking Time: 45 minutes   Serves: 6–8

gather

220g (7 oz) coffee sugar crystals or demerara sugar
100g roasted macadamias, roughly chopped

180g (¾ cup, 6 oz) dark cooking chocolate, chopped
125ml (½ cup, 4 fl oz) pouring cream
110g vanilla sugar
4 egg yolks
6 egg whites
icing sugar to serve

125ml (½ cup, 4 fl oz) pouring cream
250g (1 cup, 8 oz) dark cooking chocolate, chopped
20–40ml (1–2 tablespoons) liqueur (e.g. Frangelico) or spirit (optional)

thickened cream to serve

create

Preheat oven to 200°C (400°F, Gas Mark 6).

Praline: Combine sugar with 1 cup of water in a saucepan and stir over medium heat until sugar dissolves. Bring to boil and cook without stirring for about 20 minutes, until golden. Remove from heat and immediately pour over macadamias on a lightly oiled tray. Cool for 10–15 minutes. Break praline into large pieces and place in a plastic bag. Wrap in a tea towel and crush praline into small pieces.

Butter a 20cm (8 inch) soufflé dish, sprinkle with vanilla sugar and tie a folded piece of baking paper around dish to form a collar.

Combine chocolate with cream and sugar in saucepan and stir over medium heat until well combined. Remove from heat and cool for 5 minutes. Beat egg yolks into mix.

Whisk egg whites until stiff peaks form. Stir praline and 1 cup of egg whites into chocolate mixture, then carefully fold in remaining whites.

Spoon mixture into prepared dish and bake in the centre of the oven for 40 minutes or until well puffed.

Remove collar and serve immediately, dusted with icing sugar, with cream and chocolate sauce if desired. (This is made by combining cream, chocolate and liqueur until chocolate is melted and sauce is smooth and glossy.)

feast

A lavish sexy dessert to indulge the senses.

sticky date puddng & butterscotch sauce

Preparation Time: 20 minutes   Cooking Time: 45 minutes   Serves: 6–8

gather

Pudding

340g (11¼ oz) fresh dates
¼ teaspoon bicarbonate of soda
120g (3¾ oz) butter
170g (5¾ oz) castor sugar
4 eggs
340g (11¼ oz) plain flour
2 teaspoons baking powder
250ml (1 cup, 8 fl oz) milk

Sauce

400g (13 oz) brown sugar
250g (1 cup, 8 oz) butter
250ml (1 cup, 8 fl oz) cream

create

Preheat oven to 180°C (350°F, Gas Mark 4).

Cover dates with water and boil for 2–3 minutes. Remove from heat and add bicarbonate to water. Allow to cool completely then drain excess liquid.

Cream butter and sugar well in a mixer. Add baking powder to flour. Add one egg to mix then a quarter of the flour. Repeat until all the flour and eggs are combined.

Stop the mixer and fold dates in with a spoon. Add milk and fold.

Oil moulds before filling with mix (any size of ovenproof glass, ramekin or coffee cup can be used). Cook in a bain-marie (see page 29) for 45 minutes or until cooked—firm to touch with a spring-back feel.

For the butterscotch sauce, combine and heat sugar and butter until hot. Add cream and stir, do not boil. Allow to cool.

feast

Turn out the pudding on a plate and cover with butterscotch sauce. This is easily reheated in a microwave oven if necessary.

apple berry nut crumble

Preparation Time: 30 minutes Cooking Time: 60 minutes Serves: 12–14 **Vegan**

gather

Filling

10–12 Granny Smith apples, cored and sliced

125g (½ cup, 4 oz) apple juice

60g (¼ cup, 2 oz) almonds, chopped

60g (¼ cup, 2 oz) pine nuts

60g (¼ cup, 2 oz) hazelnuts, chopped

125g (½ cup, 4 oz) brown sugar

125g (½ cup, 4 oz) raspberries

125g (½ cup, 4 oz) blueberries

1–2 punnets strawberries, quartered

Topping

500g (2 cups, 1.1 lb) rolled oats

200g (7 oz) brown sugar

125g (½ cup, 4 oz) Nuttelex, melted

125g (½ cup, 4 oz) coconut

100ml (3½ fl oz) apple juice

create

Preheat oven to 180°C (350°F, Gas Mark 4).

For the filling, combine all ingredients and distribute evenly on a baking tray.

For the crumble topping, combine oats, coconut and sugar in a bowl. Melt Nuttelex then add to dry ingredients. Mix thoroughly and add apple juice.

Spread crumble topping evenly over filling. Bake in oven for an hour.

feast

Frozen mixed berries (bought in 1kg packets) also work well in this recipe if fresh berries are not available or in season.

pear & hazlenut tart with orange cream

Preparation Time: 30 minutes Cooking Time: 45 minutes Serves: 6–8

gather

Pastry

375g (1½ cups, 12 oz) plain flour

125g (½ cup, 4 oz) butter, chopped

2 egg yolks

1 tablespoon iced water

Filling

4 eggs

2 tablespoons brown sugar

2 tablespoons honey

1 teaspoon grated orange zest

125ml (½ cup, 4 fl oz) cream

250g (1 cup, 8 oz) hazelnuts, finely chopped

6-8 large pears

30ml (6 teaspoons, 1 fl oz) lemon juice

Orange Cream

350ml (1½ cups, 12 fl oz) orange juice

70g (2¼ oz) castor sugar

1 tablespoon arrowroot (optional)

1 tablespoon water (optional)

60ml (¼ cup, 2 fl oz) Cointreau or Grand Marnier (optional)

125ml (½ cup, 4 fl oz) cream

1 teaspoon grated orange zest

create

Preheat oven to 180°C (350°F, Gas Mark 4).

To make the pastry, sift the plain flour into a bowl, then rub in butter until mix resembles dry breadcrumbs. Add egg yolks and enough water to mix to a firm dough.

Turn onto a lightly floured surface and knead into a smooth round. Cover and refrigerate for 10 minutes.

Grease and flour tart tins. Roll out pastry and cut to size. Bake blind (see page 37) for 10–12 minutes. Remove and cool completely.

For the filling, process eggs in a blender and add sugar, honey and orange zest. Pulse. Add cream and hazelnuts and process for 30 seconds.

Pour filling mix into pastry cases and bake until slightly set.

For the sauce, heat orange juice in a small saucepan, add castor sugar and stir until thick and syrupy (use arrowroot and water paste to thicken if required). Add Cointreau or Grand Marnier if using, stir in and allow to cool. Beat cream and grated orange zest until soft peaks form, then fold into cooled orange sauce to create a luscious orange cream.

feast

Serve tart on a plate with a fanned pear brushed with lemon juice and a plentiful dollop of whipped orange cream.

chocolate macaroons

Preparation Time: 20 minutes Cooking Time: 20–25 minutes Serves: 15 **Gluten-free**

gather

300g (1¹⁄₃ cups, 10 oz) dark chocolate, roughly chopped
3 egg whites
125g (½ cup, 4 oz) castor sugar
1 vanilla bean, scraped or
1 teaspoon vanilla essence
500g (6 cups, 18 oz) coconut, long thread
100ml (3½ fl oz) milk

create

Preheat oven to 170°C (330°F, Gas Mark 4).

Melt chocolate and milk over double-boiler or in microwave and allow to cool but not re-set.

Beat egg white until stiff peaks form then add sugar, one quarter at a time. Beat continuously until sugar has dissolved before adding next quantity of sugar.

Add seeds from scraped vanilla bean or essence if using.

Fold in cooled (but not set) chocolate and coconut.

Portion onto greaseproof paper—a full teaspoon at a time—and bake until crisp on the outside but soft in the centre.

feast

These are great anytime, and they store well in an airtight container.

viennese lime biscuits

Preparation Time: 20 minutes   Cooking Time: 15 minutes   Serves: 15 (or a full hit for 1 biscuit lover!)

gather

220g (7 oz) unsalted butter, softened
125g (½ cup, 4 oz) icing sugar, sifted
3 limes, zested/grated and juiced
1 tablespoon cornflour
250g (1 cup, 8 oz) self-raising flour
icing sugar, extra

60g (¼ cup, 2 oz) unsalted butter, softened
250g (1 cup, 8 oz) icing sugar, sifted
20ml (1 tablespoon, ½ fl oz) lime juice
2 limes, zested/grated

a piping bag with a star tube

create

Preheat oven to 180°C (350°F, Gas Mark 4).

Cream butter and sifted icing sugar until soft and creamy. Add grated lime rind and juice as required to make a smooth consistency. Combine cornflour and self-raising flour, sift and add gradually, one-third at a time, until well combined.

Fill a piping bag with a star tube and pipe onto lightly greased and floured oven trays. Bake for 15 minutes or until pale golden brown. Cool on a wire rack.

Make the filling by creaming together butter, icing sugar and lime juice into a smooth thick paste.

Assemble each biscuit by spreading one with the lime filling and topping it with another biscuit. Dust finished biscuits with icing sugar.

feast

These biscuits store well in an airtight container if they are not all eaten first!

country carrot cake

Preparation Time: 20 minutes   Cooking Time: 35–40 minutes   Serves: 8

gather

250g (1 cup, 8 oz) carrots, grated and squeezed
200g (7 oz) tin crushed pineapple, very well drained
250g (1 cup, 8 oz) plain flour
1 teaspoon baking powder
¾ teaspoon bicarbonate of soda
½ teaspoon ground cinnamon
180g (¾ cup, 6 oz) castor sugar
2 eggs
100ml vegetable oil
60g (¼ cup, 2 oz) walnuts, chopped

60g (¼ cup, 2 oz) butter
60g (¼ cup, 2 oz) cream cheese
½ teaspoon vanilla essence
250g (1 cup, 8 oz) icing sugar
chopped walnuts to decorate

create

Preheat oven to 180°C (350°F, Gas Mark 4).

Mix together in a bowl the flour, baking powder, bicarbonate of soda, cinnamon and sugar. Add the eggs and oil and mix thoroughly. Stir in the grated carrot, pineapple and walnuts.

Pour into a greased ring tin or a 22cm (9 inch) round cake pan. Bake for 35–40 minutes.

For the icing, combine butter, cream cheese, vanilla essence and sifted icing sugar in a bowl and mix thoroughly until cream cheese is smooth. Add milk if too thick or more icing sugar to thicken as required. Spread icing over the cake when cooled and decorate with chopped walnuts.

feast

You will love the refreshing addition of pineapple in this cake!

monte carlo biscuits

Preparation Time: 15–20 minutes   Cooking Time: 15 minutes   Serves: 15

gather

Biscuit

185g (¾ cup, 6¼ oz)
unsalted butter
125g (½ cup, 4 oz)
castor sugar
1 egg
1 teaspoon vanilla
500g (2 cups, 1.1 lb)
plain flour
2 teaspoons baking powder
125g (½ cup, 4 oz)
desiccated coconut

Filling

60g (¼ cup, 2 oz) butter
180g (¾ cup, 6 oz) icing
sugar
2.5ml (½ teaspoon) vanilla
40ml (2 tablespoons,
$1^{3}/_{5}$ fl oz) milk
raspberry jam

create

Preheat oven to 180°C (350°F, Gas Mark 4).

Cream butter and sugar until light and fluffy. Add egg and vanilla and beat well. Add dry ingredients and coconut.

Drop spoonfuls onto a greased and floured tray. Press down with fork to shape top of biscuit. Bake in oven for 10–15 minutes until golden. Remove from oven and cool.

Create the filling by beating sifted icing sugar, butter, vanilla and milk into a thick paste.

To assemble, spread one biscuit with jam and a second biscuit with the icing mixture and sandwich the two together.

feast

Once you try these delicious homemade biscuits, you will never eat store-bought again!

orange & almond cake with citrus sauce

Preparation Time: 15 minutes   Cooking Time: 20 minutes   Serves: 4–6   **Gluten-free**

gather

Cake

2 large oranges (valencia or seedless)
250g (1 cup, 8 oz) sugar
250g (1 cup, 8 oz) slivered almonds, toasted (or almond meal)
1 teaspoon baking powder
6 eggs

Sauce

250ml (1 cup, 8 fl oz) orange juice
1 lime, juiced
1 teaspoon arrowroot

create

Preheat oven to 180°C (350°F, Gas Mark 4).

Butter and flour a 23cm (9 inch) square or round deep cake pan or individual cupcake moulds.

Cook the whole oranges, fully covered in water, in a saucepan for 1 hour. Add water as required. Allow to cool then blend whole oranges (skin and all) in a food processor.

Add all the other ingredients to the orange puree and blend again.

Pour the resulting thick batter into the prepared tin/moulds, ensuring that you mix frequently to distribute ingredients for more consistent results.

Bake for about 20 minutes. Leave the cake to cool in the tin before attempting to either turn it out or cut it.

For the sauce, blend a little orange juice and arrowroot. Heat 100ml of the orange juice and lime juice in a saucepan with the arrowroot and mix until thickened. Add more juice, depending on your preferred consistency.

feast

This gluten-free (flourless) cake will surprise many, as it uses the whole orange and almonds to give substance to the mix. Serve hot or cold with citrus sauce.

white & dark truffles

Preparation Time: 1 hour + setting time   Cooking Time: 15 minutes   Serves: 6

White Truffles

250g (1 cup, 8 oz) white chocolate

2 teaspoons arrowroot

½ teaspoon honey

50ml (¹/₅ cup, 1¾ fl oz) milk

3 egg yolks

125g (½ cup, 4 oz) unsalted butter, creamed

60ml (¼ cup, 2 fl oz) Cointreau (optional)

1 orange, zested and finely diced

125g (½ cup, 4 oz) double cream

Dark Truffles

250g (1 cup, 8 oz) dark chocolate

2 teaspoons arrowroot

1 tablespoon cocoa powder

½ teaspoon honey

50ml (¹/₅ cup, 1¾ fl oz) milk

3 egg yolks

125g (½ cup, 4 oz) butter, creamed

60ml (¼ cup, 2 fl oz) Frangelico (optional)

50g (1¾ oz) hazelnuts, finely chopped

125g (½ cup, 4 oz) double cream

125g (½ cup, 4 oz) dark chocolate

40ml (2 tablespoons, 1³/₅ fl oz) milk

double cream to serve

For each mixture:

Chop chocolate, place into a bowl and add arrowroot, honey and milk. Melt over hot water or in the microwave in 5–10 second bursts, then stirring until all the chocolate is melted through into a smooth mixture.

Add cocoa powder to dark chocolate mixture.

Allow each mixture to cool before adding beaten egg yolks (or they will cook), mix thoroughly.

Fold in creamed butter. Fold in liqueur (optional but recommended). Fold in orange zest to white chocolate mix and hazelnuts to the dark chocolate mix. Finally, fold in double cream and allow to set in refrigerator.

To make the chocolate sauce, combine dark chocolate with milk and melt in microwave (in short bursts). Allow to cool.

To serve, use an ice-cream scoop to create a ball of each truffle mix and place on a plate. Pour chocolate sauce over dark truffle and pour double cream over white truffle and serve. Garnished with mint sprigs, strawberries or orange peel if desired.

three chocolate terrine with orange syrup

Preparation Time: 1 hour   Cooking Time: 15 minutes   Serves: 12

gather

Terrine

80g (2¾ oz) dark chocolate, broken into pieces

1 teaspoon dutch cocoa powder

3 teaspoons arrowroot

6 tablespoons milk

3 tablespoons runny honey

80g (2¾ oz) milk chocolate, broken into pieces

80g (2¾ oz) white chocolate, broken into pieces

6 egg yolks

250g (1 cup, 8 oz) unsalted butter, softened and creamed

300ml (1¼ cups, 10 fl oz) double cream, whipped

Syrup

1 teaspoon arrowroot

300ml (1¼ cups, 10 fl oz) freshly squeezed orange juice

50gm (1¾ oz) sugar

125ml (½ cup, 4 fl oz) pouring cream

orange segments and mint sprigs for garnish

Line up three bowls if using a microwave or three saucepans as double-boilers.

Into one bowl, put dark chocolate, 1 teaspoon arrowroot, 2 tablespoons milk and 1 tablespoon honey.

Into the second, put the milk chocolate, 1 teaspoon arrowroot, 2 tablespoons milk and 1 tablespoon honey.

Into the third bowl, put the white chocolate, 2 tablespoons milk and remaining teaspoon of arrowroot and tablespoon of honey.

Mix all ingredients well then melt each mix in microwave or over boiling water in a saucepan, stirring constantly. Bring to the boil then remove from heat and continue to stir until cool

When cooled, beat 2 egg yolks into each mixture (making sure the egg yolks are 'thread-free'). Set aside to cool.

Blend butter in a food processor until light and fluffy. Fold one-third of the butter into each mixture, then fold in one-third of the whipped cream. (Don't overmix when folding in the cream—streaks don't matter).

Line a terrine dish with greaseproof paper. Drop in a tablespoon of white chocolate first then a tablespoon of dark chocolate then a tablespoon of milk chocolate. Repeat until base is covered, starting with dark chocolate first on this layer and milk chocolate first on the next layer, ensuring mix is evenly distributed for colour and flavour.

Refrigerate overnight or place in freezer. Turn out, cut and serve.

To make the syrup, mix the arrowroot with a little of the orange juice until smooth. Put in a pan with the remaining juice and sugar and stir over heat until boiling. Simmer for 2 minutes, then cool.

Refrigerate until ready to serve, then drizzle slices with orange syrup and decorate with fresh orange segments and mint sprigs.

First published in Australia in 2010 by
New Holland Publishers (Australia) Pty Ltd
Sydney • Auckland • London • Cape Town

www.newholland.com.au

1/66 Gibbes Street Chatswood NSW 2067 Australia
218 Lake Road Northcote Auckland New Zealand
86 Edgware Road London W2 2EA United Kingdom
80 McKenzie Street Cape Town 8001 South Africa

National Library of Australia Cataloguing-in-Publication entry

de Ath, Adam.

Harvest Vegetarian / Adam de Ath.

1st ed.

ISBN: 9781741109030 (hbk.)

Vegetarian cookery.

641.5636

Publisher: Fiona Schultz
Publishing manager: Lliane Clarke
Project editor: Helen McGarry
Designer: Amanda Tarlau
Photography: Graeme Gillies/NHIL
Cover photograph: Graeme Gillies/NHIL
Stylist: Trish Heagerty
Production manager: Olga Dementiev
Printer: Toppan Leefung Printing